PLANTING A WATER GARDEN

By Dr. Joseph L. Thimes

Quarterly

yearBOOKS, INC.
Dr. Herbert R. Axelrod,
Founder & Chairman

Dominique De Vito
Chief Editor

yearBOOKS are all photo composed, color separated and designed on Scitex equipment in Neptune, N.J. with the following staff:

DIGITAL PRE-PRESS
Patricia Northrup
Supervisor

Robert Onyrscuk
Jose Reyes

COMPUTER ART
Patti Escabi
Sandra Taylor Gale
Candida Moreira
Joanne Muzyka
Francine Shulman

ADVERTISING SALES
Nancy S. Rivadeneira
Advertising Sales Director
Cheryl J. Blyth
Advertising Account Manager
Amy Manning
Advertising Director
Sandy Cutillo
Advertising Coordinator

©yearBOOKS, Inc.
1 TFH Plaza
Neptune, N.J. 07753
Completely manufactured in
Neptune, N.J. USA
Designed by Sandra Taylor Gale
Cover design by Sherise Buhagiar

INTRODUCTION

This short book, PLANTING A WATER GARDEN, describes a step-by-step format on how a beginner can get started in and successfully grow water lilies. The three major phases in water gardening are planning, construction, and maintenance of your pool. Lack of information on costs in water gardening literature is a big disappointment to me. It practically does not exist. At the end of certain chapters and at the end of this book, costs that I found in the summer of 1996 are given. I have included a short chapter on the history of water lilies for general information. In general, I would recommend a beginner to start with a tub or kettle-like water garden as these are the easiest in effort to start with and the least expensive in costs. If one likes the results and wants to expand, then proceed ahead at an acceptable pace. Then, if possible, don't skimp on the size of your pool.

What are Quarterlies?

Because keeping Water Gardens is growing at a rapid pace, information on new equipment, new varieties and prices are vitally needed in the marketplace. Books, the usual way information of this sort is transmitted, can be too slow. Sometimes by the book is written and published, the material contained therein is a year or two old…and no new material has been added during that time. Only a book in a magazine form can bring breaking stories and current information. A magazine is streamlined in production, so we have adopted certain magazine publishing techniques in the creation of this yearBOOK. Magazines also can be much cheaper than books because they are supported by advertising. To combine these asstes into a great publication, we issued this yearBOOK in both magazine and book format at different prices.

CONTENTS

Topics included in this book are planning, type of pool, tubs and kettles, new pool consideration, ideal ratios of plans and animals for your pool, suppliers and equipment, year-round maintenance, winder precautions, storing of plants over winder, fish, types of water lilies and other plants recommended, etc. Outside the scope of this book are pool construction, circulating systems and filters, fountains, and other complex equipment. For those beginning in water gardening, the best of luck and much enjoyment to you!

Lastly, I appreciate the help that Mr. Ken Landon, a well-known water lily developer from San Angelo (Texas), Mr. Ted Lannan of Lincoln (Nebraska), and Earl May Nursery in Omaha (Nebraska) gave to me when I was writing this book.

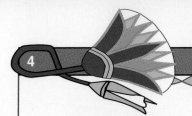

HISTORY

ANCIENT EGYPT

From ancient Egypt, the original concept of beauty comes from the graceful curves of the lotus plant. The earliest depiction I found on the lotus was a drawing of two queens of the great pyramid builders (about 2500 BC) picking lotus blossoms while on a boating expedition. In the ancient Egypt of the era of Ramses II (about 1250 BC), the lotuses were in fact the true water lilies: *Nymphaea caerulea,* the BLUE lotus known for its fragrance and in art, and *Nymphaea lotus*, the WHITE lotus often used at banquets. In hieroglyphics, SESHEN was the word denoting the lotus blossom.

In religion, the lotus was a symbol of creation and resurrection, served in solemnities of the gods, participated in funerary rites, and was an ingredient in sacred waters. As sacred waters, the lotus-tinted waters were used in purification rituals of priests, as votive offerings to the divinities, and in blessing the earth. In funerary observances, the lotus blossom provided sustenance for the survivors. Sometimes, the petals of the blue lotus accompanied the mummies of the pharaohs. According to the most venerable of legends, a huge lotus emerged from the primeval waters and gave birth to the sun. This sun was seen rising like a hawk from the lotus bud. One famous piece from Tutankhamun's tomb clearly displays this creation theme.

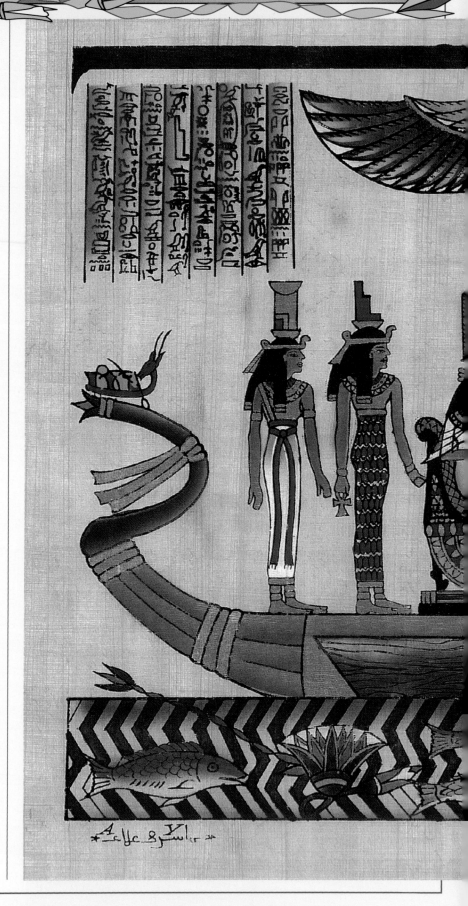

Lotus blossoms are featured throughout this ancient Egyptian scene depicting life in Egypt around 1200 BC, or 3200 years ago!

This Egyptian gentleman is royalty. He holds a lotus blossom in his left hand with lotus buds decorating the ritual cups on a table in front of him. This dates about 1500 BC.

At festive banquets, white lotuses adorned the hair of many fair maidens and served as necklets on many young dandies. Banquet guests often placed blue lotuses to the noses to smell their sweet fragrances.

In ancient Egyptian art, the placement of the lotus blossom is of utmost importance. If the blossom is UPRIGHT especially with an aquatic setting, rebirth or creation themes are intended. If the blossom is shown SIDEWISE, human usage is depicted. If the blossom is INVERTED or upside down, only decorative usage is meant. In art, lotus flowers can be found on golden chalices, alabaster oil lamps, mirrors, faience or ceramic bowls, drawings in tombs and on papyrus and limestone, in huge pillars of temples, on the golden mask Psusennes I, and in many intricate jewelry pieces. In the renowned exhibitions of both Tutankhamun and Ramses II, many pieces showing lotuses were displayed. In the Ramses II exhibit, I remember vividly the golden lotus chalice of Queen Tausert (about 1200 BC) and a blue faience bowl of lotuses with fish.

Many parts of the lotus plant were used. Of course, the blossom was the main attraction in art, religion, and festivities. The golden array of the stamens reminded ancient Egyptians of the golden rays of the sun. The large lotus pads provided shade for fish in the Nile River. For food, the rhizomes were ground into "flour" for use in bread and served as a source of starch in nutrition.

From the blue lotus (*Nymphaea caerulea*), both *Nymphaea blue beauty* (also known as *Nymphaea pennsylvania*) and *Nymphaea daubeniana* are derived. These are day-blooming tropical water lilies. From the white lotus (*Nymphaea lotus*), many of the flat-opening night bloomers were developed, including *Nymphaea wood's white knight*. These are night-blooming tropical water lilies.

From ancient Egypt, lotus lore spread to many countries including Phoenicia, Israel, Assyria, Persia, Greece, Rome, India, China, and Japan. Hindu creation myths contain much parallelism with the venerable ancient Egyptian creation myths. In architecture, the lotus pillars of Egypt influenced the columns of both Solomon's Temple and the Ionic style of the Greeks.

PALESTINE AND THE BIBLE

On the tomb of Ahiram of Byblos in Phoenicia, this king is shown holding a lotus blossom. The king would physically resemble the famous King Hiram of Typre, friend of Solomon. In several places in the Bible, lotuses are mentioned. In King Solomon's era (about 1000 BC) two huge temple pillars were lotus shaped. The modern names Susan and Suzanna (in Hebrew, "Shûwshan" or "Shôwshannâh") mean the white lotus! Recently, some exquisite ivory peices from King Ahab's capital city of Samaria (about 850 BC) had lotus motifs.

ASSYRIA AND PERSIA

From the lotus of Egypt, the Assyrian sacred tree, the "tree of life," often displayed lotus buds and rosettes. Many Assyrian ivory pieces from Nimrod depicted lotus themes.

From the tomb of Nakht, 18th Dynasty Egypt, this extremely well preserved drawing shows a bearer holding a bouquet of three lotus blossoms in his right hand while his left hand holds other offerings with a hanging of grapes.

These are scenes from the Valley of the Nobles, about 3200 years ago, depicting the journey of the corpse of Kiki to Abidos. The funereal boat carrying the mummified Pharaoh is decorated with lotus blossoms.

About 450 BC, Persia introduced the true pink lotus, *Nelumbo nucifera*, to ancient Egypt. This beautiful bloom became very important in the Ptolemaic art of Egypt (300 to 30 BC) and also became the sacred lotus of Asia.

GREECE AND ROME

In architecture, the Egyptian lotus capitals, the top part of pillars, formed the basis for the IONIC style of Greek columns. On various vases from Rhodes, Crete, and Greece, lotus flowers can be found. On some Roman mosaics, lotus blooms are clearly shown. Today, water lily blossoms are grown in pools located at the Vestal Virgin House on the Roman Forum.

HINDUISM

In the Hindu creation saga, Vishnu, the protector of the world, was seated on the multi-headed cobra, Ananta, which was a symbol of eternity. Ananta was floating on an ocean of infinite milk. From Vishnu's belly, a lotus blossom emerged. Upon this blossom, the Brahma is seated. The Brahma proceeded in the work of creation. This parallels the ancient Egyptian creation myth.

BUDDHISM

About 550 BC, Prince Siddhartha, who was later known as Buddha, was born. At his conception, lakes and ponds were filled with lotuses. At the moment of Buddha's birth, a lotus appeared wherever Buddha touched the world that day. He took seven steps. Today, many Buddhists place lotus offerings at their shrines as a symbol of purity. The lotus position, Padmasana, is the yoga posture of meditation. The true pink lotus, *Nelumbo nucifera*, is the sacred lotus of Asia today.

MODERN HISTORY

A modern revival in water lilies occured in the 1800's in Europe. The spectacular Victoria amazonica of South America was discovered in the early 1800's. In the 1890's, William Tricker became the first grower of tropical water lilies in the United States. In 1901, Claude Monet created his water lily pond in Giverny, France. Later, he immortalized water lilies in his famous paintings. In the early 1900's, Latour Marliac hybridized hardy water lilies to obtain exotic colors of yellow, pink, and red. Marliac hybrids are well known today, and these hybrids can withstand harsh winters. In 1906, George Pring came to America and became the superintendent of St. Louis's Missouri Botanical Garden for many years. He developed the well known St. Louis cultivar in 1933. In about 1977, Leicester Thomas founded Lilypons Water Gardens in Maryland. He named this water garden after Lily Pons, the famous French opera singer. Well known modern water lily hybridizers include Perry Slocum, Dr. Kirk Strawn, Jack Wood, Martin Randig, and Ken Landon. In modern water lily language, hybrid water lily plants are known as "cultivars."

From the Tomb of Sennifer, a domestic scene shows a husband and wife sailing down the Nile River while a servant offers them food. The wife has a lotus blossom in her right hand.

PLANNING

Planning the water lily garden is the first and perhaps the most important step in the decision-making to build the water lily pool. In the planning stage, one should look at many factors including total costs involved, choice of location and type of pool, winter precautions needed, appropriate plants including water lilies, and equipment desired. Start small by using a whiskey barrel or a kettle pool to see if you enjoy growing water lilies. This would keep the expenses down, require one to use minimal planning and effort, and enjoy the water lilies themselves. In addition, these tubs or kettles could be used as decorative containers for land plants or even indoor marginal water plants if one did not like growing water lilies. Planning gives one a chance to look at the whole picture of costs, efforts, time needed, and materials involved in order to get into water gardening.

POOL LOCATION

Choosing the right spot is a most important decision in designing a water garden. Installing a water garden is a big job. Moving one is next to impossible.

As water lilies need much sunlight, the site should be one that receives at least 4 to 6 hours of direct sunlight per day. If possible, place the water garden in such a position where one can observe it from several strategic viewing points such as from upstairs, kitchen,

A plastic-lined pond, with waterfalls, decorative rock edges, equipment enclosures, stone lantern, bench lighting and other decorative features shown along with the diagram of the filtration and water treatment system.

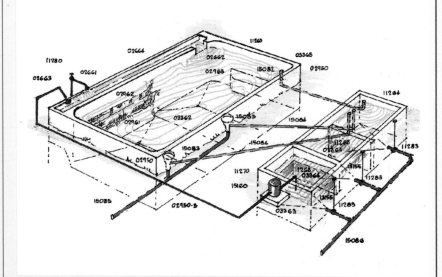

This pond is a composite showing the main pond elements. These include the feeding shelf, plant shelf, plant shelf with screen guard to protect young leaves from koi chewing them, rectifier drains to separate debris from clear bottom water, fresh and processed water supply, filter tank connections and drainage piping, overflow, and aerating water.

Both drawings by Andre Benoist from *THE ATLAS OF GARDEN PONDS (TFH number TS-178)*. The numerals are architect's numerals the translation of which can be found on page 279 of the above referenced book.

living room, porch, or patio, etc. This location should be close to a water supply like a garden hose. Place the water pool on level ground or ground that can be easily leveled. A non-level pool is very undesirable for esthetics. Never place such a pool in a low-lying area that collects water as these areas often accumulate water filled with debris and contaminants. If possible, locate the pool AWAY from trees. In general, trees (1) provide shade to the involved areas, which interferes with needed sunlight, (2) drop leaves, which become debris at the pool's bottom, and (3) can provide roots, which can prevent excavation of the pool or damage a pool liner at a later time. If pumps, lights, and other electrical devices are to be used, then suitable electrical outlets should be located nearby. If one lives in a cold winter climate, one should consider using windbreaks such as solid fences or evergreen shrubs to reduce the effects of the icy Northern winds. If one is excavating for a water garden, one should locate water, gas, and electrical utility lines, and septic tank pipes first. If in doubt, contact the appropriate utility companies involved.

SHAPE AND SIZE OF POOL

The shape of the pool should harmonize with the entire water garden area

A garden pond that was surrounded with trees until their overhanging branches were sawed off. This pond belongs to Minoru Kawaguchi. It has a surface area of about 5,000 square feet. Photo courtesy of Zen Nippon Airinkai.

A carefully planned water garden around which there is plenty of vegetation but little overhang. This is a small pond of barely 100 square feet. It belongs to Kyutaro Nakui. Photo courtesy of Zen Nippon Airinkai.

which is a very integral part of the entire landscape.

If starting with a pool larger than a tub or kettle, one should decide on a reasonable number of plants to grow. When building a pool of this size, don't be stingy on the dimensions of the pool. After many people build a smaller sized pool, they often decide to build a larger pool later on. The total expense of building two pools would be much more than building a larger

pool in the first place. Remember that the larger the pool is, the less susceptible that pool will be to environmental factors.

CLIMATE

The type of climate one lives in has much to do with plant selection, maintenance, equipment, and winter precautions.

In plant selection, the colder climates can limit the types of plants one grows. For

example, very cold weather might preclude the growing of tropical water lilies. In humid, hot climates, growing of some hardy water lilies can be limited.

In general, climate can have much to do with pool design, equipment, maintenance, and winter precautions. In colder climates, pools should be constructed deeper to prevent the complete freezing of water in winter. Also, pools should be constructed stronger to

withstand the effects of expansion when water turns into ice. In colder climates, more equipment is sometimes needed and more precautions for winter must be implemented.

EQUIPMENT, SUPPLIES, AND SUPPLIERS

In planning, one should consider the total supplies and equipment needed. If excavating a pool, one should consider who would do the excavation, how the

Above: Mr. Shuko Yamaguchi located his pond in the shade of large trees. This is very dangerous and requires constant cleaning. The alternative is to have water moving quickly over the surface of the pond, recirculating it through a filter. Photo courtesy of Zen Nippon Airinkai. Below: To completely control all environmental factors, Shigeo Ishikawa converted his swimming pool into a koi pond! It has about 200 square feet of surface area. Photo courtesy of Zen Nippon Airinkai.

excavation should be done, the amount of flexible liner for the pool to be used or type of rigid pool needed, and types of plants desired. In general, most water lily pools need very little equipment if properly thought out and maintained. Finally, one should look into the suppliers available in his or her locality to provide the needed supplies and helpful advice. Obviously, your local pet shop is your best source for supplies and information. Mail order firms are your worst source.

COSTS

In building water gardens, one should have an overall idea as to the maximum amount of money to be spent which would be acceptable to the family budget. Then, one should check into various suppliers as to actual prices for the supplies, equipment, and construction needed. When the total reasonable costs are obtained, one should compare these costs to the amount allowed in the budget. If the total expenses are within the budget, then one can feel comfortable with starting the project. If the total costs are NOT within the budget, one should consider possibly down-sizing the proposed water garden project.

MAINTENANCE

The best way to keep maintenance to a minimum is to plan a correct ideal ratio of water lilies, other plants, and fish. Once the ecosystem of the pool is balanced, the water garden will be essentially self-sustaining. Do not oversupply the pool with plants, fish, or snails.

Above: Mr. Ryohei Fujisawa built his water garden inside his home. It has a surface area of 400 square feet and has a depth of 4-6 feet. He has no algae problem and, therefore, has a very small filtering system. Photo courtesy of Zen Nippon Airinkai. Below: Masafusa Hamada owns this immaculately conceived garden pond decorated with surrounding evergreen bushes and trees. This is an extremely expensive pond to build and maintain as the bushes and trees must be manicured regularly. Photo courtesy of Zen Nippon Airinkai.

Above left: The location. Above right: The concrete collar method is to lay a concrete base upon which to set the edging after the pond is lined. Be sure to level the collar as this level will determine the depth and drainage of the pond water.

Above left: Ready to start the digging. Above right: You need help! Invite the neighbors, your friends and the kids! Below left: The first step in the installation of the bottom drain. Below right: Completing the installation of the bottom drain.

Above left: The outlet and intake lines of the filter system are VERY important to the future operation of your pond. Above right: Check the sides and bottom for sharp objects and roots.

Above left: One inch of sand is laid for additional protection. Above right: Unfolding the liner, one fold at a time, does not disturb the sand base. Above right: The liner is carried to the pond and placed in position. Bottom right: Screwing the top collar into the bottom drain.

Above left: The magic moment...adding the water. Above right: Cutting away the excess liner.

Above left: Laying out the edging..remember...lay out first, rearrange, then, when you are satisfied with the layout, mortar it in. Above right: Mortaring the liner in. Once it is in it is too late to make changes. Below left: Finished! Below right: Planted!

The same site one year later.

LARGER POOLS

Pools come in many shapes and sizes. For small pools such as tubs and kettles, half whiskey barrels, wash tubs, steel tanks, and small pre-formed pools work well. For larger pools, these are usually of three types: concrete, rigid, and flexible liner types. Some of these pools can be built above ground.

PLANNING

When building a larger pool, extra considerations other than in the planning chapter should be taken into consideration. I would check into local zoning laws concerning fencing of pools. In some localities, pools that are 24 inches or more in depth must be fenced. Another item to check on is the purity of the water supply in your area. Chlorines and chloramines do cause problems for a pool, as do other contaminants. In the proposed site where one wishes to build, check for large boulders, tree trunk root obstructions, septic tanks, and utility (electrical, gas, water, sewer) lines, etc. If the obstructions are too great, choose another location. If your site is good, consider how the main construction will be done. Are you capable of doing this work yourself or will you need outside help to complete the construction? A good starting size is usually anywhere between an 8-foot by 6-foot size to about a 15-foot by 10-foot expanse. Remember that the larger pools will resist environmental stresses much more than smaller pools.

CONCRETE POOLS

Concrete pools are the most expensive to build and are outside the scope of this book. However, if building this type of pool, be sure to use a good reinforced concrete of appropriate thickness (usually 4 to 6 inches or more) to withstand winter's harshness. Obtain an experienced

This pool, measuring about 10 x 24 feet, is made of concrete and belongs to Tadashi Tanishiga It is completely enclosed, thus requiring only a very small filtering and water cleansing system. Photo courtesy of Zen Nippon Airinkai.

contractor to construct this type of pool. If possible, check into the credentials of such a contractor and examine some examples of his work.

RIGID POOLS

Usually, these pools are either of fiberglass or HDPE (High Density Polyethylene). In many cases, HDPE is black in color. These pools are often

1/4 to 1/5 of an inch in thickness or more. In many cases, these pools can be bought at hardware stores, local nurseries, and national water lily suppliers. "Mac Court" is the brand name for very available HDPE pools. Prices for these rigid pools vary from about $100 to $1,000. There are thinner,

small pre-formed "shell" pools which can work like a tub or kettle pool.

FLEXIBLE LINER POOLS

Usually, flexible liner pools are made using liners of PVC (polyvinyl chloride), EPDM (ethylenepropylene diene monomer), and polyethylene. If possible, obtain a black or dark gray liner as these colors give a sense of depth to the pool. If using a flexible liner, make the liner dimension per length or width about 3 to 4 feet more than the corresponding length or width of the pool plus twice the depth of that pool. It is safer to have a little excess of material on hand than to be too short on material. If too short of flexible liner, one has simply wasted expense on the original amount ordered and then must reorder a larger amount for the pool.

For flexible liner pools, several suggestions should be made. First, at least one side should have a shelf about 1 foot deep and 8 to 12 inches or more wide. This shelf serves several purposes: (1) allowing an ideal planting depth for many marginal plants, (2) permitting an escape pathway for small children, pets, and other people falling into the pool to be in effect, (3) easing work in lifting heavy plant containers into and out of the pool, and (4) allowing one to enter and exit the pool much more easily to do required maintenance work. Secondly, if possible, plan to have one side 4 to 6 inches deeper than the other sides. Having this deeper side serves two purposes: (1) ease in cleaning the pool and (2) providing a protective deeper area for your plants and fish in the winter. If one is draining the pool, it is simple to "force spray" the debris to this deepest side. Then, the removal of this debris is much simpler as the debris is concentrated on that one side. If needed, I'd recommend sloping the sides of the pool to ease the

Above: Rigid pools sunken into the ground can be very unique. The owner, Shigenori Tashima, produced 500 square feet of surface using four rigid fiberglass ponds. They are set into the ground, at ground level, and have removable screen covers to protect people and animals from falling into the water which is 6 feet deep. Photo courtesy of Zen Nippon Airinkai. Below: This pond, belonging to Dr. Yukio Abe, is only 180 square feet with 4 feet of maximum depth. It is built under a cover. The PVC liner can be held down with large stones uniformly placed around the periphery of the pond. Photo courtesy of Zen Nippon Airinkai.

ABOVE GROUND INSTALLATION OF A FIBERGLASS POND
Photos by Anita Nelson.

Above left: The site prior to preparation. Above right: Leveling the fiberglass pool. Note the concrete slab in the background. This will be used for the filtering system.

Above left: Preparing the site. Above right: Building up the background with cinder blocks. This also provides a platform for the waterfalls. Below left: The rocks have been delivered and the preparation for the filter installation has commenced. Below right: The rocks are laid out first, to be sure they fit and are aesthetically acceptable, before they are cemented in position.

Mayla, a magnificent hardy water lily. Photo by Anita Nelson.

Laying in the filter lines.

Scrubbing the mortar joints with vinegar to neutralize the lime in the concrete.

The job is done! Wasn't it worth the effort?

pressure of expansion when water turns into ice in the winter. Such linear expansion of 3 percent can create tremendous pressure against the sides of the pool. If possible, don't skimp on the size of a flexible liner pool. Harmonize the shape of this pool with your nearby surroundings.

ABOVE GROUND POOLS

An above ground pool can be built using either landscape ties or 4-inch by 4-inch wood beams held together in place by either using solid metal rods like "rebar" or by construction cinder blocks. Usually, the 4-inch by 4-inch wood beams can be found in longer lengths than the landscape ties. A flexible liner (usually of EPDM or PVC) is used to line the pool.

An above ground pool (background) converted to a garden while the semi-submerged pool continues to thrive. These pools belong to Dr. Herbert R. Axelrod.

In the Singapore airport there is a koi and water lily pond set on top of the floor. It is not too successful as the light is not strong enough for the lilies.

GENERAL CONSIDERATIONS

The flexible liner pools seem to be the most popular today; and EPDM seems to be the material of choice as it is black in color, tough, durable, and rubber-like in consistency. Its thickness often runs from 40 mil to 73 mil with 45 mil (45 mil = .045" = 45 thousandths of an inch) size being the most popular. Local suppliers include hardware stores, roofing supply houses, and local nurseries. Many national water garden suppliers carry this material as well. Oftentimes, local roofing suppliers are the least expensive in price. PVC liners are also readily available. Polyvinyl chloride (PVC) is more commonly known simply as "vinyl." PVC liners typically run 20 to 32 mil in thickness.

CONTRACTORS

Construction of such pools is outside the scope of this book. However, for use of flexible liner, rigid, or concrete pools, excavation is usually necessary. If one can do the excavation himself with a shovel, wheelbarrow, etc., one can save a lot of money. If you can't do the work, contact a local excavator, gravel company, general contractor, or nursery to see who performs this work in your area. I found such costs to run about $30 per man-hour from a local nursery. This local nursery could construct the entire pool for you—including all materials. Check on the sand, pea gravel, dirt, and decorative rock for the pool. A layer of damp sand will help stabilize the pool in its final resting position. A protective layer of cardboard, foam rubber, or rug padding should be used to protect a flexible liner from puncture due to such sharp objects as stones or tree trunks. A 2- to 3- inch layer of damp sand or dirt should be placed between this protective layer and the flexible liner. Be absolutely sure that the top edges of the pool are level! Flagstone, decorative rock, bricks, logs, etc. can be used to accent the pool's outer dimensions.

ELECTRICAL

Using electrical equipment in or near the garden pool requires extreme caution to prevent electrical injuries, including electrocution. One excellent method is to use a ground fault circuit interrupter, which can cost about $65 to $70. If in doubt, consult an electrician or electrical supply company.

OTHER POOL IDEAS

Family wading pools are a possibility to get started in a larger pool. I have seen a 12-foot in diameter by 3-foot deep pool lined with thick blue vinyl liner for about $150 at a large discount store. Spare pool liners for this pool run about $50 apiece. This pool is collapsible and easily stored in the winter time. Also available is an 8-foot in diameter by 18-inches deep plastic pool for $19. This smaller pool is very susceptible to punctures. The key point to remember is that some of these pools' vinyl might be harmful to fish and water plants. If you are interested in any of these pools, be sure to check on possible toxicity of the vinyl or plastic materials involved.

TYPICAL COSTS	
Small Backhoe (L)	$160 - 200 per day
Excavation Labor (L)	$30 per man hour
Decorative Rock (L)	10 to 22¢ per pound
(depends on color)	
Dirt (L)	$12 per cubic yard
Sand (L)	$16 per ton
Pea Gravel	$37 per ton
EPDM Flexible Liner (L)	55¢ - $1.38 per sq. ft.
(45 mil)	(N) 73¢ - 99¢ per sq. ft.
PVC Flexible Liner (L)	75¢ per sq. ft.
(20 mil)	(N) 63¢ - $1.05 per sq. ft.
PVC Flexible Liner (32 mil) (N)	81¢ - 85¢ per sq. ft.
NOTE: 1 ton above = 100 square foot area by 2 inch deep layer	

Mitsunori Hasuda built this above ground pool and sheltered it, thus depriving the pool of enough light to grow lilies. But the covering does keep the water clean even with minimum filtration. Photo courtesy of Zen Nippon Airinkai.

In general, if you start your water garden in the spring, you should have a thriving garden by summer. These are Louisiana Irises. Photo by Rich Sacher.

PROBLEMS WITH NEW POOLS

In general, new pools should be started in the springtime. When the pool is ready, fill it with water and let this water sit in place for a few days. Then stock the pool with your plants. Let these plants stay in the pool for a couple of weeks alone. The submerged plants will be supplying oxygen to the water. After about two weeks or so, fish and snails can be safely added to the water. Algae will cause the water to turn green! This is a natural occurrence for any new pool started, and in each springtime for established pools. It usually takes from two to eight weeks for the pool to take control of this algae. Especially in warmer climates, the murky water can last longer. The key point here is to be patient and do nothing. Your water garden pool will arrange the ecosystem participants in a natural relationship with each other to create a near-perfect balance which will make a delightful scene! Never change the pool water at this point. If you change the water at this point, you will have to RESTART the entire water balancing processes all over again.

If the murkiness continues, check for two things: (1) overfeeding the fish or (2) too many fish. If overfeeding your fish, simply avoid feeding your fish for 2 to 3 weeks. If too many fish is the problem, you could give some of the fish away, provide more submerged plants, or possibly move your submerged plants closer to the surface of the water so that they can produce more oxygen. This should stop the algae. If not, check on the ratios of your plants and fish.

TUB AND KETTLE TYPE POOLS

When starting tub water gardens, start small. Many items that serve well as garden pools include wood tubs, whiskey half barrels, galvanized or plastic trash cans, large crock pots, sinks, certain laundry baskets, steel tanks, 55 gallon drums, large plastic drums or flower pots, kettles, horse troughs, small pre-formed plastic pools, dipping tubs for dogs, and old bath tubs. Any of these should be scrubbed thoroughly with clean water first. If possible, stay away from detergents. If detergents are used, then be sure to scrub your container thoroughly to eliminate all traces of detergent.

If wood containers such as whiskey half barrels are used, special care must be given to the wood. Wood containers often have preservatives in them that are harmful to plants and animals. As untreated wood will rot quickly when it comes in contact with water, I would treat this wood with wood preservatives. Polyurethane "paint" will protect the wood such as the staves in a whiskey half barrel. Protect all sides of the wood with these preservatives. However, as mentioned before, these preservatives are harmful to fish and plants. To create a safe environment for your plants and fish in your wood

The typical wooden whisky half barrel. Photo by the author.

pool, line the wood pool with an appropriate liner of PVC, EPDM, or polyethylene. It is this liner that protects your fish and plants from the preservatives.

If your container is metal, paint the insides of that container with an appropriate rubber-based paint. This paint is readily available locally and will make most metal containers safe for your plants and fish. Be sure to let this paint dry thoroughly and set. You could also line metal containers with PVC, EPDM, or polyethylene liner. Some people have successfully lined metal containers using large plastic bags. If using these bags, be sure that water does not contact the inside metal.

Once cleaned, large ceramic pots, large crock pots, plastic containers, and fully porcelain-lined metal containers should be safe to use.

SPECIFIC TUBS AND KETTLES

For tubs, I will limit discussions to whiskey half barrels which are about 24 inches in diameter, 16 to 17 inches tall, and about 3 square feet in water surface area. For kettles, I am referring to those of 36 inches in diameter and about 7 square feet of water surface area.

Whiskey half barrels can easily be lined with various liners of PVC, EPDM, or polyethylene measuring about 4 feet by 5 feet. There is, however, a much easier way! I'd recommend using a pre-formed plastic whiskey barrel liner for this. This pre-formed liner not only serves as an

excellent liner but also holds the wood whiskey barrel together. At local nurseries, both the whiskey barrel and the pre-formed liner run about $25 each. Hence, the whiskey barrel set-up would run about $50. Both the properly lined whiskey barrel and the polyethylene barrel work well.

Careful attention should be placed on the location of your tub garden. A key factor is to place the tub in a position that protects it against the hottest 2 to 3 hours of sun per day. Partial shade at this time works well. This will

Small, pre-formed HDPE (plastic) pool. Photo by the author.

moderate the differences of water temperatures during the hottest and the coolest parts of the day and helps prevent the tub's water from overheating. Remember, however, that water lilies require a good amount of sunlight. If sunlight may be a significant problem, choose the most shade-tolerant of water lilies and marginal plants for your pool. If possible, keep the tubs off of the grass as this could cause unsightly discoloration in the grass. Place the tub in such a position so that the top rim is perfectly level. Shims placed

on the bottom of the tub may be needed to level out the tub's top surface. I'd recommend keeping this tub or kettle above ground. However, the tub or kettle can be submerged into the ground. If this is done, treat any wood in this tub with a wood preservative first to slow down the wood rotting process.

When filling the tub with water, let this water stand for 2 to 3 days before putting the plants in. This allows the chlorine in the water to dissipate. Use of plastic containers to place individual plants is recommended. These plants should be in the tub about 1 to 2 weeks before the fish and snails are introduced. Mosquito fish (*Gambusia affinis*) are excellent fish for warmer climates. Feeder goldfish can also be used - especially in cooler climates. Be careful not to overfeed your fish in a tub or kettle. During the week, the water should be topped off at least twice to replace the water volume lost due to evaporation. If possible, let the water to be added stand for awhile until its temperature equals the water temperature inside the tub. Then, add this needed water. This will minimize the chances of shocking the fish with sudden temperature changes. Another way to add water would be to very slowly add this water in a thin stream to the tub. The chlorine in this water will help control algae in the tub.

Usually, the tub's ecosystem will balance out within 60 days.

When draining such a tub, special precautions should be used - especially when the tub is a wooden whiskey half barrel. Remember that the filled tub is heavy! Tipping a wooden whiskey half barrel causes strains that stress the integrity of that barrel. Regular siphons can be used to drain such a tub. Here, one can use suitable tubing or an appropriate length of garden hose as the siphon. The key is to submerge the entire tubing into the tub and let this tubing completely fill with water. Then plug one end of the tubing. Remove the other end of this tubing and place this end BELOW any portion of the tub. Then, remove the plug. Let the siphoning proceed. Whenever siphoning be sure to use precautions for your fish. In some limited types of larger pools (especially in above ground larger pools), this siphoning procedure will work. Bailing out water by pans will also work.

Tubs create an almost carefree atmosphere in performing water gardening. No weeding and no spraying is needed. However, small amounts of regular maintenance still need to be done. This includes plant fertilization, rhizome division, and some winterization procedures. In winter, many marginal plants make ideal indoor house plants. These tubs and kettles can be brought indoors if desired. If this is done, drain the tub water into another container and move the tub inside. Then, when the tub's top edge is again perfectly level, place the original tub water back into the tub. A regular workman's level will work well to obtain a perfectly level top surface for your tub.

Ideal ratios for tubs and kettle are given below:

PLANTS FOR TUBS AND KETTLES

For tubs and kettles, hardy water lilies that are especially good include: Chromatella (yellow), Pink Beauty or Fabiola (pink), Helvola (miniature yellow), Hermine (white), Aurora (changeable yellow to red), and Gloriosa (red). For kettles in warmer climates, Texas Dawn (yellow) is outstanding. For cooler climates, I'd recommend starting with one of these hardies as these are the easiest to grow. While the Helvola is the most tolerant to shade, both the Hermine and the Texas Dawn perform well in partial shade.

For tubs and kettles, the tropical water lilies easiest to grow include: Dauben (light blue), Colorata (blue) are great while Panama Pacific (rich violet) and Madame Ganna Walska (striking violet-pink) work well. St. Louis Gold will work well in kettles. While the Dauben is the most tolerant of shade, Panama Pacific, Colorata, and Madame Ganna Walska do well in partial shade.

Certain lotuses are grown successfully in tubs and kettles. These lotuses include: Tulip or Shirokunshi (white), Chawan Basu (white to cream with pink edges), Momo Botan (red), and Baby Doll (white). There are some people who can grow the sacred pink lotus (*Nelumbo nucifera*) in a tub. However, I think it would be best to save this exquisite and large lotus for medium to large pools.

For those beginning in water gardening in tubs, I would recommend starting with a dependable, proven species of hardy or tropical water lily. The hardy type is more easily grown in general than the tropical type. I would tend to stay away from the lotus or try the lotus last.

For marginal plants in tubs and kettles, I'd most strongly recommend dwarf papyrus, dwarf or regular umbrella palm, some taro, arrowhead, water iris, Sagittaria, and smaller varieties of cattails. For submerged plants, I'd recommend Elodea to provide oxygen to the water. Water lettuce would be my choice as a floating plant. These plants are described in another chapter.

For animals, I'd recommend either mosquito fish or feeder goldfish and ramshorn snails as my scavengers. An aerating pump might be needed to supply oxygen to the pool - especially when the weather is very hot.

Unless the local nursery has one of the mentioned water lilies (or lotuses) in this chapter, I would recommend ordering your specific and desired species from a national water garden supplier. Often times, their prices on specific and proven species are very attractively priced. A listing of some of these suppliers is given in the SUPPLIERS SECTION. Marginal, submerged, and (in some cases) floating plants can be obtained from these same national suppliers.

Nymphaea gigantea, the blue Australian water lily. Photo by Anita Nelson.

However, I prefer ordering these marginal, submerged, and floating plants from a local nursery as a person can view these plants and buy only the most physically attractive plants. Order your plants very specifically, and costs can be kept reasonably minimal when doing so. Order your fish and snails from a reputable and local fish (or pet) store. Again, here, one can choose attractive fish and snails to buy.

The larger kettles and tubs provide more surface area of water to grow plants in. This can be a decided advantage as more dependable water lily species can be found. In the water lilies I mentioned, the Texas Dawn and St. Louis Gold will grow nicely in kettles.

COSTS

Wood Whiskey 1/2 Barrel & Liner (24") (L) .... $50.
Polyethylene 1/2 Barrel (24") (N) .... $30-$33
Leerio Patio Tub (30")(N) .... $59.
Square Tub (26-27" per side)(N) .... $45.
Patio Tub (32")(N) .... $59.
Kettles (36")(N) .... $90-$135
Wheeled Storage Unit (45 Gal.)(L) .... $30-$35
(Euro-Blue in color)
(dimensions about 35"L x 19"W x l7.5"Tall)

SURFACE AREA
In Square Feet
1/2 Barrel (24") 3.14
Leerio Patio Tub (30") 4.91
Patio Tub (32") 5.59
Square Tub (26-27" per side) .... 4.80 (Avg.)
Kettle (36") 7.07
Wheeled Storage Unit (35" x 19") .... 4.62 (Est.)

This is a small, pre-cast concrete pool that is available as a wading pool for children, or for several other purposes. Swimming pool suppliers, plumbing suppliers and concrete contractors should be contacted with the hope they have something that might suit your needs. Photo by the author.

ENVIRONMENTAL FACTORS

After the pool construction is completed, the key point is to start with a balanced ecosystem and to keep that ecosystem balanced. One should obtain a general idea of the topic of photosynthesis in order to understand how environmental factors work. By knowing the contributions that appropriate plants and animals make towards the ecosystem, one can plan how to arrive at a good balance between these living entities. Finally, ideal ratios for these plants and animals are given so that one can start with a workable balanced system. In this chapter, environmental processes, contribution plants and animals, water purity, and ideal ratios will be discussed.

PHOTOSYNTHESIS

In photosynthesis (the making of food by using light energy by plants), light energy is converted into chemical energy which is stored as food (sugars) in green plants. Plants combine carbon dioxide (CO_2) and water (H_2O) to produce food ($C_6H_{12}O_6$ as sugars) and give off oxygen (O_2) as a waste product. In respiration, plants and animals "burn" the food with oxygen to release energy needed for growth and other life functions. In respiration, plants and animals combine food and oxygen to produce energy while releasing carbon dioxide and water as waste products. In short, respiration is simply the reverse of photosynthesis. The complete cycle of photosynthesis and respiration maintains the earth's natural balance of carbon dioxide and oxygen.

In the water garden, the main participants of the effective photosynthesis-respiration cycle are the submerged (or oxygenating) plants and fish. Here, the submerged plants use light to combine carbon dioxide and water to produce food and give off oxygen. This oxygen is consumed by fish in breathing. In this cycle, fish give off carbon dioxide as a waste. This carbon dioxide is picked up primarily by the submerged plants and algae. This consumption of the carbon dioxide by the submerged plants and other nutrients by the floating plants helps keep the troublesome algae under control.

Of course, all green plants participate in photosynthesis. However, marginal plants, water lilies, and floating plants use mainly carbon dioxide from the air - not the carbon dioxide from the water.

The other cycle that figures in on the ecosystem balance is the nitrogen cycle. Nitrogen fixing (or nitrifying) bacteria convert free nitrogen (N_2) of the atmosphere and decaying matter into usable nitrates for plants. If the nitrifying bacteria of the water garden are wiped out, the pond will become defenseless against organic wastes.

The excrement from the fish are eaten by the scavenging snails.

CONTRIBUTING PLANTS AND ANIMALS

The submerged plants, a key contributor, are also known as oxygenating plants. They keep the water clean and compete against the troublesome algae for the same nutrients. Through photosynthesis, submerged plants produce oxygen for the fish and snails to consume. These submerged plants absorb carbon dioxide from both fish wastes and from decaying matter. These plants combine this carbon dioxide with water to produce food needed for plant growth. If these submerged plants consume enough carbon dioxide, they make it tough for the competing algae. Their foliage serve as a spawning ground for fish and as a food for fish.

Floating plants serve to purify water by removing many impurities and pollutants. In fact, in some water reclamation centers, these floating plants are used as nature's way to purify water. These floating plants compete against algae for many of the same nutrients. One floating plant can do the work of several submerged plants in purifying the water.

Marginal plants are also known as bog or accent plants. Their main purpose is to provide the finishing touches to a perfectly balanced water garden. As great ornamental plants, many put on a good show all summer and can be sensational indoor plants in water. Marginal plants live in shallow water.

Peter Nelson sits on the leaf of a Victoria Longwood. Photo by Anita Nelson.

In our water gardens, the water lily is our star performer and serves as an outstanding ornamental water plant. In regular sized pools, about 60% surface coverage by water lily pads is considered excellent. The coverage by the pads cools and shades the water. In addition, these pads help minimize the water's oxygen loss and decrease the evaporation of water. This pad coverage also helps to control the algae.

pool, and other refuse in the pool.

An excess of algae signifies a gaseous problem such as low oxygen content. Nature's way to control algae is to use proper water lily pad coverage and to use a good supply of both submerged and floating plants. Algae likes to use carbon dioxide of the pool. Remember that algae blooms in all new pools and each spring in established pools. This is normal.

an "Alka Minus" type of solution to lower the water pH to near 7.0. If the pH level is under 6.0, use an "alka Plus" type of solution to raise the pH reading to near 7.0. Typically, these solutions run about $10 to $13 per 16 fluid ounces. Various pH adjusters are available at every aquarium pet shop.

Nitrogenous wastes such as ammonia, nitrates, and nitrites are sometimes encountered when a new pool is set up or after some chemical treatments. In some cases, certain fish medications can kill the beneficial nitrifying bacterial population. If these useful bacteria are wiped out, the garden pool is rendered defenseless against organic wastes. If using fish medications, check with the local fish shop on how to use these chemicals without destroying the nitrifying bacteria. Certain bacterial additives are restorers of such nitrifying bacteria and are supplied by the major water garden suppliers. Nitrogenous waste test kits are reasonably priced. In addition, heavy metal and phosphate removers are available.

A major contaminant is chlorine. If chlorine is a problem, find out if the offender is free chlorine or is chlorine. Check with your local water department to see exactly what type of chlorine is used. When adding a large amount of water to the pool (as in starting a new pool, etc.), let the water stand for 3 to 4 days. This will allow the free chlorine to dissipate from the water. Usually, this makes

A small water lily pool belonging to Gary and Cindy Gabelhouse of Lincoln, Nebraska. It is completely covered with lilies and Water Hyacinth, which makes the algae suffer from lack of light. Photo by the author.

Fish are often called the "gardeners" of the water garden. They consume oxygen produced by the plants and also dine on such pests as aphids, flies, and mosquito larvae. These fish help complete the photosynthesis-respiration cycle.

Snails, the scavengers of the water pool, eat algae off plants and plant containers. They also consume fish excrement, decaying matter such as fallen leaves on the bottom of the

WATER PURITY

In general, ideal water should have a low level of contaminants, experience no sudden temperature changes, be neutral in pH, and have a proper oxygen level.

Ideally, water should have a neutral pH of about 7.0. If the water's pH is <u>NOT</u> between 6.0 and 8.0, the pH level should be corrected. Simple pH test kits and paper testing strips are readily available. If the pH level is over 8.0, use

the water safe for the fish and the plants. If free chlorine is the problem, use chlorine neutralizers. However, if chloramine is the offender, different treatments are needed as chloramine is much more toxic to the fish. Sometimes, chloramine neutralizers are effective against either free chlorine or nitrogenous wastes. The best advice is to know what the offending contaminant is, then buy the neutralizer effective against that contaminant, and then use this neutralizer in a correct way. Usually, one can safely add up to about 5% of pool volume of water into the pool at one time without hurting the fish or plants. This untreated water should be added SLOWLY to minimize sudden temperature changes. In fact, such water added often acts as an algaecide and fungicide.

Chemical treatments for algae (algaecides) are also on the market. The best way is to avoid chemicals here if possible because a properly balanced pool will naturally keep algae under control. Algae growths in new pools and in the springtime in established pools are natural occurrences and should subside in a few weeks.

In general, a well-balanced pool will keep the water relatively free of contaminants. So, stay away from chemical treatments if possible. If an emergency exists, however, test to find out what offending problems exist. Then, take appropriate action to correct these problems. If chemical treatments are indicated, use the correct chemicals in a correct way.

Water oxygen levels are important to the fish. Too low an oxygen content in water will stress the fish and can cause their death. Remember that warm water will hold less oxygen than cold water. Also, oxygen is depleted at night. If low oxygen content in water is a problem, consider buying an aeration pump for your pool. Then, use this pump at night and in hot weather. Too much plant life might be another reason for low oxygen content. Ideal ratios should help in determining if this is a problem. Sometimes, adding more submerged plants will help in correcting a low oxygen content in water.

IDEAL RATIOS

Ideal ratios are approximate starting figures to achieve a well-balanced ecosystem as soon as possible. Ideal ratios consider the various types of plants

COSTS

pH Adjusters (16 fl. oz.) (N) .... $10-$13
Bacterial Additives (12 fl. oz) (N) $20
Chlorine Neutralizers (16 fl. oz) (N) .... $11-$18
Chloramine Neutralizers (16 fl. oz) (N) .... $12-$14
Ammonia Neutralizers (nitrogen neutralizer) (N) .... $8-$12
Water Test Kits (but not for ammonia) (N) $20
Ammonia Test Kit (N) $7
Chloramine/Chlorine Test Kit (N) $14
Aerating Pump (N&L) (N) .... $45-$50

Nymphaea lotus variety *dentata*, the White Lotus of Ancient Egypt. The blossom to the right is a young blossom; an older blossom is on the left. Older blossoms have stamens further apart and are less fresh-looking. Photo by the author.

and animals to use. Generally, it is best to start with a good supply of submerged and floating plants to compete against algae and to provide a good oxygen content to the water. On the other hand, it is best to start with an undersupply of fish because too many fish will upset the ecosystem. Fish will increase their population to a suitable number for your pool later on. Water lilies should be chosen to provide about 60% water surface coverage with their pads. Here, ideal ratios are for larger-sized pools. The figures below are good starting approximations.

Contributor	(per 10 ft²) (or per 1 m²)	(per 100 ft²) (or per 10 m²)
Submerged plants (in bunches) (1 bunch = 6 stems)	4 - 6	50 - 100
Floating plants	2	15 - 25
Marginal plants	2 - 3	15 - 20
Water Lilies (depends on species)	1	5 -10
Fish (in inches)	4-- 2" OK 10 in. max	100" - 150" max
Snails	6 - 9	50 - 80

The author, Joseph L. Thimes, at the Swift Family Garden Pools in the Missouri Botanical Garden, St. Louis, Missouri.

PRACTICAL TIDBITS

In the spring and summer of 1996, I visited the water garden pools created by Ted Lannan in Lincoln, Nebraska. He is very practical, is skilled in construction, and keeps his costs to a minimum. His ideas may help you in keeping expenses down. He has built three pools with the smallest being 8 feet long by 4 feet wide and the largest being an oval 20 feet long by 15 feet wide.

He excavated his pools himself and used odd pieces of carpet remnants and padding as a protective liner against sharp objects. He recommended obtaining the carpet and carpet padding from neighbors moving out of their homes or at apartment complexes. These can be obtained at very low or even at no cost to you! Mr. Lannan carefully removed all tacks from this padding in order to prevent the tacks from puncturing his EPDM lining. Foam rubber also works well.

Mr. Lannan placed quartzite rock over his lining. To do this, he helped local farmers remove boulders from their land. In short, this rock was free to him! Other sources for this rock are at gravel suppliers, local nurseries, and nearby quarries. For the large pond, he completed the outside portion of the pool by using tree logs for a natural look. For the small pool, flagstone was used. Cost involving rock can be a significant water garden expense. For EPDM lining, he found a suitable supply from a roofing supply company for just under 40

Above: An EPDM (plastic) lining in a medium-sized pool, 8 feet square, belonging to Ted Lannan in Lincoln, Nebraska. The hole has been dug, the liner is long enough, and the stones are being arranged to line the pond. Photo by the author. Below: Ted Lannan finished this medium-sized pool, 8 feet square. The progress is shown above. A few water lettuce plants are floating in the pond already! Photo by the author.

Above: This pool was made from a large, flexible liner (EPDM plastic). It belongs to Ted Lannan of Lincoln, Nebraska and is 20 x 8 feet. Photo by the author.

Above: A typical hardy water lily that Ted Lannan grows in Lincoln, Nebraska. It gets very cold in Nebraska during the winter. Photo by the author. Below: Ted Lannan built this small water lily pond. It is 4 x 8'. Photo by the author.

centers per square foot for a 500-square-foot roll. Smaller pieces were at 60 cents per square foot.

For equipment, Mr. Lannan bought a stock tank bubblizing machine from a farm supply dealer. He uses no pool heater in Nebraska's harsh and cold winder. This machine supplies oxygen to the pond during the year and helps maintain an ice-free portion of the pond in winter to provide for an exchange of gases. He uses two pumps to recycle water through the large pool and the stream leading to this pool.

For streams, Mr. Lannan recommends using 45 mil EPDM liner and to keep the stream area as shallow and as wide as possible. He uses a layer of gravel on top of this stream. For this stream, use of a single EPDM piece is the best. If not available, the liner sheets should be overlapped.

In general, Mr. Lannan uses arrowheads and cattails as his marginal plants and Elodea as his submerged plants. For the small pool, he used an airplane plant to accent the pool. Plastic pots are used to contain his plants. For lotuses, he uses heavy clay soil with no manure. For his water lilies, he uses river rock gravel. His water lilies consist of local varieties that grow in the wild in the midwest. Regular water lily fertilizer tables are used 2 to 3 times per year for both water lilies and lotuses. A natural look for his larger pool was a key goal. In the fall, he cuts the vegetation off the water lilies and lotuses and lowers these containers to the

Above: The Earl May Nursery in Omaha, Nebraska, constructed this large flexible liner (EPDM) pond on their property as an above ground water garden. Photo by the author. Below: Typical hardy water lily grown by Gary and Cindy Gabelhouse in Lincoln, Nebraska. Photo by the author.

deepest part of the pool where they stay for the winter. In the spring, rhizome division is performed. Mr. Lannan has grown water lilies in his large pool for 5 years.

His largest pool is an oval measuring 20 feet in length, 15 feet in width, and 2 feet in depth. He has a ledge (or shelf) around the pool set at a 1 foot in depth level and 18 inches wide. Rocks line the walls and shelf of this large pool. To keep a natural look, tree trunk logs line the edges of this pool; wildflowers provide some of the background. For fish, small bass and bluegills are used. To control algae, a one-foot-long oriental grass carp (amur) is used. This fish costs about $10 from a local fish store. In 1996, he had about 20 water lily plants and one lotus in the pool. He plans to reduce the water lily plant total to about 10 to 12 plants. Cattails and arrowheads serve for decorative purposes, and Elodea provides oxygen to the pool.

The smallest pool measures 8 feet long by 4 feet wide. Regular goldfish reside there. For plants, small water lilies, an airplane plant, and a small arrowhead are in this pool.

Mr. Lannan's friends, Gary and Cindy Gabelhouse of Lincoln, were the ones that gave him the spark in developing water garden ponds. The Gabelhouses grow regular papyrus and large taro plants as marginal plants in their pools. In addition, they have an excellent supply of water hyacinths and water lettuces on hand. For floating plants, they now prefer water lettuces.

FISH AND SNAILS

When starting a new water garden, it is recommended starting with small "feeder" goldfish (*Carassius auratus*) as these fish are inexpensive and hardy. To begin with, use an undersupply of fish. For larger pools, a good figure is about 1/3 to 1/2 inch of fish per square foot. The fish will expand in numbers and size to reach a healthy fish population for your pool. Other fish worth looking into are the mosquito fish (*Gambusia affinis*) and guppy (*Poecilia reticulata* - in older books = *Lebistes reticulatus*). Minnows can also work well. Buy only healthy fish having clear eyes, clean skin, non-frayed fins, and active swimming habits. In a garden pool as well as in an aquarium, fish will provide hours of enjoyment with their graceful swimming. The ideal fish for large ponds are Japanese colored carp (Koi).

Fish are considered the "pond gardeners." They will eat submerged plants such as Elodea, mosquito larvae, insects, and some algae. In addition, they consume oxygen produced by plants.

When introducing fish to a new pool, carry them home in a plastic bag filled with water from the local fish store. Protect the bag against the hot sun by covering it with a newspaper or towel. When you arrive at your water garden, place the floating bag on the water and then cover this bag with a newspaper to prevent the sun from overheating the bag. Float the

You don't want to use goldfish that are too fancy, as they cannot compete for food or get protection against larger fishes. This two-color Ryukin goldfish is just the thing for the small pond. Photo by Fred Rosenzweig.

bag in the water until the bag's water equals the pool's water temperature. This bag floating usually takes about 1 hour. This method prevents sudden temperature changing shock to the fish and minimizes problems in fish handling. Remember when feeding the fish, feed them **SPARINGLY**. Fish dine on insects, mosquito larvae, leaf miners, aphids, and submerged plants. When feeding fish, feed for only 5 to 10 minutes or until the food begins to sink. Use only a floating type of fish food such as fish pellets. Daphnia and grubs could be used on occasion.

There are many kinds of mosquito fish (so-called because they eat mosquitoes and mosquito larvae). These are *Gambusia puncticulata*. Photo by Andre Roth.

As fish are hardy and adaptable, they will survive winters, provided that a portion of the water surface is kept continually free from ice. In colder climates, the pool should be at least 24 inches deep. If the water is considered dangerous to the fish, consider either using aerating pumps and/or de-icer machines to keep an ice-free portion at the water's surface or bring the fish indoors into suitable aquariums.

Your local pet shop has many kinds of guppies. Get those with short fins as they do best in ponds, but they usually cannot take temperatures below 60°F. Photo by Tanaka.

If your water garden has collected too much debris, clean the pool out. Usually, springtime is the best time to clean the pool. When cleaning the pool, consider the health of your fish. First, fill large containers such as large buckets or tubs, etc. with the pool's water. Using small fish nets or pails, capture the fish and transport them to the above containers. Here, the fish will be transported to water that they were used to; and this water in the container should be at the same temperature as that of

Left: A kinginrin showa sanshoku koi of champion quality. Photo courtesy of Zen Nippon Airinkai. Center: The most popular of koi is the kohaku, the red and white koi. This is a champion quality fish. Photo courtesy of Zen Nippon Airinkai. Right: A kinginrin shiro utsuri of championship stature. This fish is 28 inches long and is a female, that's why she's so thick. Photo courtesy of Zen Nippon Airinkai.

the remaining pool water. Finish cleaning the offending debris from the pool's bottom. After this is done, fill the pool with water via your garden hose and let this water stand for an hour or two until the temperature of the new pool's water equals the container's water temperature. If the new water needs to be treated with anti-chlorine chemicals, do so now. The last step is placing the fish into the new water of your pool.

Fish stress is caused by poor water quality and by the handling and transport of fish. If the cause is by handling, symptoms of fish stress usually occurs within 2 to 3 weeks.

There are many fish diseases such as fin and tail

Dr. Axelrod's book on *HEALTHY POND FISH* is a must for everyone keeping fishes in their garden ponds. The official number is TFH YB-102. It is available at all pet shops and garden centers which are serious about water garden supplies.

rot, white spot disease, parasites, fungus, etc. When the fish are sick, consult with your local fish store, giving that store the exact symptoms and history of your fish. These stores will have appropriate fish disease remedies on hand. Often, parasites can be removed from fish by simply using tweezers. Dr. Axelrod's book of pond fish diseases is indispensable for every water gardener.

SNAILS

Snails are considered the "pond's scavengers" as they eat algae from submerged plants and plant containers, eat decaying matter and dead leaves, and consume fish excrement. The right snails are the "ramshorn" (genus

Planorbis) and black Japanese (*Viviparis malleatus*) snails, which do the above tasks without harming the plants. Ramshorn snails have flat, dial-like circular shells.

When introducing snails to your pond, rinse them with pond water and slip them into the pond. The living snails will sink while the dead snails float. Simply remove the floating snails. It takes about one week for the snails to recover from being added to the pool.

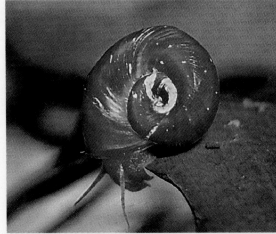

Left: The water garden snail, *Planorbis*. Below: The black Japanese snail, *Viviparis malleatus*.

PESTS

For aphids, simply spray the affected areas with your garden hose to knock these aphids off the plants and into the water. The fish will finish the job for you! Fish will also control other nuisances such as leaf miners, mosquito larvae, and other offending insects.

COSTS	
Feeder goldfish (inexpensive)(L)	20¢-30¢
Snails (Ramshorn)(N)(for 6 to 9 snails)	40¢- 75¢
Fish Stress Coat Treatment (16 oz.)(N)	$12
Fish (Antifungal or Antiparasitic)(20 oz.)(N)	$15-$16
Malachite Green Treatment 1 qt.)(N)	$18

Water lilies, marginal plants and pool fish are being prepared for shipping at this Ft. Myers, Florida facility. Most livestock is available year round and is shipped worldwide via air freight and courier services. Photo courtesy of Professional Aquarist. (941-543-5300)

Mosquito larvae are air-breathing aquatic insects before they become blood-sucking flying pests.

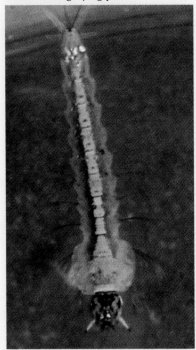

WATER GARDEN PLACES VISITED

I will describe some of the places that I have visited that have outstanding water lilies and lotuses. In addition, I have given the city locations of some of the other outstanding water lily gardens in the United States. Finally, I have given city locations of major water garden suppliers with whom I have corresponded. Often, these major suppliers have exquisite display gardens. I tried to give a good selection of sites available through the United States. There are many outstanding water lily locations that I have not listed.

SAN ANGELO, TEXAS

Located downtown in Civic League Park in San Angelo, the Water Lily Collection of San Angelo was started in 1986 by the well known water lily developer, Ken Landon. Over 50 different species of water lilies of many different colors are gown in the large pool, which is 125 feet long by 25 feet wide by 26 inches in depth.

Mr. Landon helped to develop the University of Texas collection which was the world's largest collection of water lilies in the 1970's. He has over 25 years of research experience in the water lily field and works at Olive Nursery in San Angelo. From a part of the University of Texas collection, he started the San Angelo water garden. Mr. Landon balances this collection with pure species and hybrids known as cultivars. Among the water lily

This is the large water lily pool in which Ken Landon does much of his research. It is called the *Water Lily Collection of San Angelo* in San Angelo, Texas. Photo by the author.

varieties that Mr. Landon has developed are: Texas Dawn, Rebecca Jennifer, Catherine Marie, Lemonscent, and Rhonda Kay (purple variety).

In San Angelo's pool, there is a nice balance between the hardy and the tropical varieties of water lilies as well as the magnificent Victoria longwood. Of course, the first visible blooms are of the hardy type floating on the water's surface. These blooms start by mid-April and last through the summer. The tropical blooms rising high above the water's surface

Nymphaea Rhonda Kay is a tropical water lily. This is a first day flower which extends more than a foot above the surface of the water. This variety was developed by Ken Landon.

start to show in June and last through September or October. Both of the ancient Egyptian "lotuses" can be seen in this pool. Actually, these "lotuses" are tropical water lilies - *Nymphaea caerulea*, the sacred blue lotus of the Nile *Nymphaea lotus*, and white lotus. In

Nymphaea Jennifer Rebecca is a night-blooming tropical water lily developed by Ken Landon. Photo by the author.

addition, one can view the most magnificent plant, *Victoria longwood*, in late summer. This Victoria exhibits pads that range from 6 to 8 feet across! This water lily garden in San Angelo is easily accessible for the handicapped.

In the same Civic League Park, one can view exotic rose

Nymphaea Catherine Marie, a night-blooming tropical water lily developed by Ken Landon. Photo by the author.

gardens, walk across unique stone walking bridges, and enjoy the tranquillity of riverfront and nature path walkways. In addition, many huge and majestic cypress trees line this park. Plan on spending at least 2 to 3 hours when visiting all of the sites at this park. At another downtown location, geometrically designed gardens of exotic land cannas can be viewed.

To see lotuses, you don't have to travel far to observe "fields" of the American Yellow Lotus, *Nelumbo lutea*. These blooms often measure 10 to 11 inches across with pads about 1 1/2 to 2 feet in diameter. At Lake Nasworthy in southern San Angelo, you can see many areas of this lotus. This lake is extremely picturesque and has outstanding boating and fishing facilities. You could also travel to Christoval, a small town located 17 miles south of San Angelo to see river banks filled with this delightful lotus. This river area has cooking facilities and tree ropes available for those individuals who would like to vault into the river like Tarzan. Hence, by visiting San Angelo, you can see all the major types of water lilies and lotuses ranging from the hardy variety to the tropical version to the true lotus (*Nelumbo*) to the spectacular Victoria!

MISSOURI BOTANICAL GARDENS, ST. LOUIS, MISSOURI

On Labor Day weekend of 1996, I visited the romantic Missouri Botanical Gardens encompassing 79 acres located on Shaw Boulevard in St. Louis, Missouri. This site,

The Swift Family Garden Pool at the Missouri Botanical Garden in St. Louis, Missouri. Photo by the author.

founded in 1859, features Japanese and English gardens, the "Climatron" (a tropical rain forest), rose gardens, a home gardening center, and two areas of beautiful water lilies. The famous water lily developer, George Pring, was superintendent of this center for many years. The largest area, the Milles Sculpture Gardens, features two large

Milles Sculpture Garden at the Missouri Botanical Garden, St. Louis, Missouri. Photo by the author.

rectangular pools featuring many various tropical water lilies. The large centrally located circular pool between these two large rectangular pools displays the huge *Victoria longwood* which had pads measuring about 4 feet across and large blooms. These gardens feature large bronze sculptures produced by Carl Milles. Another area displaying tropical water lilies is the Swift Family Garden

The huge leaves of the *Victoria longwood* at the Milles Sculpture Gardens. Photo by the author.

Pools. This area displays many excellent marginal plants as well as a few tropical water lilies. At the Lotus Bed area of the Japanese Gardens (an area I regret not seeing), the *Nelumbo nucifera*, known as the "improved Egyptian pink" or sacred lotus, is grown. If you visit this center on Labor Day weekend, you can observe many interesting demonstrations of the International Japanese Festival.

An arrangement of tropical water lilies at the Swift Family Garden Pool at the Missouri Botanical Garden, St. Louis, Missouri. Photo by the author.

LAKE MANAWA STATE PARK, COUNCIL BLUFFS, IOWA

In August, you can view many acres of the exquisite American Yellow Lotus, *Nelumbo lutea*. Here, the blooms often measure 10 to 11 inches in diameter and rise over 4 feet above the surface of the water. The largest pads,

The Doran Lily Pool in Gage Park, Topeka, Kansas. Photo by the author.

Huge fields of American Yellow Lotus in Lake Manawa State Park, Council Bluffs, Iowa.

Above: The author, Joseph L. Thimes, amidst a mass of lotus plants in Lake Manawa State Park. The author is standing on the bottom of the pool and there were pads 39 inches above the surface of the water. Below: *Nelumbo lutea*, the American Yellow Lotus, shown as an open blossom. Photo by the author.

shaped like inverted Chinese coolie hats or like inverted umbrellas, can measure two feet across. These pads can rise over 3 feet out of the water. The distinguishing feature of the true lotus is the golden seed pods which is shaped like a faucet "nozzle" head. Lake Manawa is located in Council Bluffs, Iowa. The best time to view these exotic lotus flowers and pads is from mid-August to Labor Day. Be careful if you try to pick the blossoms. The footing by the lotus flowers is treacherous due to several inches of quagmire.

TOPEKA, KANSAS

The Doran Lily Pool at Gage Park was developed in 1930. Its measurements are about 23 yards long by 8 yards wide. This pool displays white, pink, and yellow varieties of hardy water lilies. This pool is located in Gage Park. Park also offers beautiful rose gardens, Doran Rock Garden featuring irises and roses, Topeka's zoo, and an enclosed

The author's mother, Virginia Thimes, holding a blossom and a leaf of the American Yellow Lotus. Photo by the author.

Water lilies being grown at the Roman Forum, home of the Vestal Virgin, Rome, Italy. Photo by the author

rain forest. In the summer, huge fields of cultivated sunflowers await the viewer just outside of Topeka.

ROME, ITALY

On my trip to Rome, Italy, in October 1996, I learned that water lilies are grown in the pools located on the site of the Vestal Virgins House at the old Roman Forum. On my tour of the Roman Forum, I was able to photograph this famous historical site with the water lily pads. Though no blooms were apparent, I noticed some buds ready to rise.

SOME OTHER OUTSTANDING WATER LILY GARDENS

1. Longwood Gardens
   Kennett Square, PA
2. New York Botanical Gardens
   Bronx, NY
3. Brooklyn Botanical Gardens
   Brooklyn, NY
4. Kenilworth Aquatic Garden
   Washington, DC
5. Balboa Park
   San Diego, CA
6. Denver Botanical Gardens
   Denver, CO

EQUIPMENT

Successful water gardening can effectively be done with minimal costs and equipment. If electrical devices are used, a ground fault circuit interrupter is a necessity. An aeration pump may be worth looking into. De-icers, water removing pumps, pond sweeps, water circulation pumps, and lighting devices are described but are not necessary. The main idea of this book is to explain how a beginner can start water gardening in a practical and successful way while keeping costs at a minimum.

Expensive fountains, filters, water circulating systems, lighting systems, and water falls are not needed to begin water gardening. Hence, these items fall outside the scope of this book. They can, however, be added later on to an already successful water lily garden.

GROUND FAULT CIRCUIT INTERRUPTER

If electrical equipment is to be used in or around the pool, I'd strongly recommend using a ground fault circuit interrupter with an extension cord for safety reasons. This device shuts off the electrical current when it detects water coming into contact with the wiring. This gadget would minimize the chances of an electrical injury, including electrocution, caused by electricity contacting water. Typically, this unit costs about $50 to $70. If in doubt, have an electrician install this device.

AERATION PUMPS

Aeration pumps supply oxygen to the pool's water. This can be essential during hot weather or even possibly at night to provide an essential level of oxygen to your fish. These pumps also help in keeping a small ice-free area in a water garden in cold winters. These pumps generally cost about $50.

DE-ICER WITH GUARD

The de-icers keep about a 2-foot in diameter surface area of your pool free from ice in cold winters. This ice-free area allows for an exchange of gases in water - allowing oxygen into the pool and toxic gases out of the pool. This helps to keep your fish alive in harsh winters. The de-icers usually run about $60.

WATER REMOVING PUMPS

These pumps typically cost about $170 to $200 and remove water from the pool. You can also rent siphoning pumps from a local equipment rental store when draining the pool's water is necessary. Wet vacuum systems will also work. Bailing out the water by hand is a tedious procedure.

POND SWEEPS

Pond sweeps, also known as "pond vacs" or "leaf eaters," operate with a garden hose to create a vacuum that removes debris, such as fallen leaves, from the pool's bottom. Monthly vacuuming can remove about 70% of this debris. These pond vacs usually come with either vacuum bags or have exhaust tubing. These devices are very safe as they don't use electricity and might preclude the need of water removing pumps. Typical costs are from $27 to $85.

WATER RECIRCULATING PUMPS

If water recirculating pumps are to be used, be sure to have a pump that moves the entire pool water volume through it in less than 2 hours. This 2-hour time limit is the maximum time to be used. A pump less than this minimal capacity is NO good - a waste of money. Water recirculating pumps are not absolutely necessary and are expensive (especially when a water recirculation system is planned). These pumps are mentioned only because they are found in many pools. In a well-balanced pool, neither pumps nor filters are necessary. Most water gardeners using these pumps do use filters. The main purpose of these recirculating pumps is to improve water quality. If used, place these pumps a few inches above the pool's bottom where the water oxygen level is the lowest.

LIGHTING

Subtle, indirect, out-of-pool illumination is often the most effective. If electrical out-of-the-pool illumination is used, be sure that this system is safe and consider using a ground fault circuit interrupter. Non-electrical illumination as candles, luminaries, Tiki candles, etc.

provide an enchanting glow to a garden pool at night in a very inexpensive and safe manner. For one starting out in water gardening, I'd recommend staying away from expensive in-water illumination systems.

POND NETTING

If falling of leaves in autumn is a serious problem, a leaf-catching pond netting can help. The costs of such netting typically runs about $10 for small pools to about $35 for large pools.

LILY PRUNERS

Water lily pruners are 4-foot long pruners that allow you to trim excess or unwanted foliage from water plants. The cost per pruner is about $30 to $33. Long lopping shears from local hardware stores also work. These typically run from $20 to $25 but sometimes can be obtained for as low as $10. If one doesn't mind stepping into the water garden, you can trim away these plants at no cost by using a good set of regular scissors.

INJECT-A-TAB DEVICE

This device provides the easiest way for a water gardener to fertilize water plants using minimal effort. This instrument eliminates the lifting of heavy plant containers out of the water. These inject-a-tab tools generally cost about $30. Using a little effort, you can build this simple device by assembling PVC pip tubing, wood dowels, and nails to hold the wood dowel in place

Some ultraviolet units combine sterilization features with biological filtration, thereby purifying and clarifying the water at the same time. Photo courtesy of Ani Mate, Inc.

(averaging as little as $4 apiece; about $12 for three such tools)! The PVC tubing should be just a little larger than the lily tabs you will be using. Of course, you can fertilize water plants without this device at no cost.

SUMMARY

The general idea for a beginner in water gardening is to stay away from as much equipment as possible. Planning will allow you to do so. In general, I'd trim foliage with a good set of scissors and hand make a suitable

inject-a-tab-like instrument (or buy an inject-a-tab device). If electrical equipment must be used, invest a little money into a ground fault circuit interrupter for safety reasons. If weather conditions warrant aeration pumps or de-icers, purchase these items. Pond netting may be useful during certain times of the year. The equipment given above seems to be a reasonable expense if it is needed. In general, it is best to stay away from fancy equipment and its costs involved in the beginning.

COSTS

Ground Fault Circuit Interrupter (N)	$50-$70
Aeration Pumps(N) & (L)	$50
De-icer with Guard (N)	$60
Water Removing Pumps (N)	$170-$200
Wet Vacs (L)	$35-$120
Pond Sweeps (N)	$27-$86
Pond Netting (N) (Small Pools)	$10
(N) (Large Pools)	$35
Water Lily Pruners (N)	$30-$33
Lopping Shears (L) (as low as $10)	$20-$25
Inject-A-Tab Device (N)	$30
Handmade one (L) ($12 for 3)	$4 Average

MAINTENANCE

In general, plan maintenance to perform work practically, efficiently, and with minimal effort. Once the pool is set up, let nature take its own course. Intervene only for emergencies and for routine maintenance. A key factor in maintenance is the severity of your winters. In harsh, cold winters, special precautions are needed.

For major pool cleaning, consider springtime to do this as it seems to be the best time. The coolness of the water at this time makes it easier for fish to survive the draining of the pool's water.

When performing general maintenance in the pool, you should wear old sneakers or rubber boots or even go in barefoot. Doing this will minimize chances of tearing the pool liner when performing maintenance. When raising or lowering containers into place, use ropes placed into the drilled holes of these containers. As these containers of your plants can be heavy, two people may be needed to do this work. If the pool depth is too deep for proper container water depth level, use clean bricks or large, smooth stones underneath to raise the container to a proper water depth level.

DRAINING POOLS

If the debris on the bottom of the pool is excessive or if there is danger of most of the water freezing in harsh winters, the pool should be drained. Use pond sweeps every so often (about once a month) to reduce the debris on the pool's bottom. When the decision is made to drain your pool, take all precautionary measures to protect your plants and fish. Put some pond water into a large container. Then, scoop the fish out of the pool and place them into the temporary container. Removal of the pool's water can be done by using siphoning pumps, wet vacuum systems, bailing out water with buckets, or by simple tubing siphons in certain cases. If you can get a long piece of tubing from your pool to a lower level than the bottom of your pool, a siphon of flexible hardware tubing or garden hose can be used. Here, place the entire tubing into the pool and have it completely fill up with water. Then, plug up one end and leave this end in the pool. This plug will hold the existing water in the tubing. Remove the free end of the tubing to a lower level than the pool bottom. Remove the plug, and let the siphoning begin. If the ground is too level, then a pump, wet vacuum system, or bailing out of the water by hand must be used. Be sure to protect your fish and plants first before draining your pool.

SPRING

After the risk of cold has COMPLETELY passed, pool coverings can be removed. This will allow the pool's water to warm faster. As this water warms, algae will turn the water to a bright green color. This is a normal yearly occurrence. Make sure that all of the pool's equipment is in good working order. If needed, clean the excess debris on the pool's bottom after draining the pool's water. If draining the pool, be sure to use this old pool water on your regular gardens as this discarded water is rich in nutrients. Then, refill the pool with garden hose water and let this water stand for several days to neutralize the chlorine. If fish were removed just previously, replace such fish into your pool after the new pool's water equals the temperature of the temporary storage container's water. In this case, put these fish in as soon as possible.

Springtime is a great time to divide rhizomes and start fertilization of your plants. Divide and repot your water lilies every 2 to 3 years or when they show signs of rhizome overcrowding, such as very few blossoms. When the plants are properly potted, lower these containers to proper locations using ropes. If fish need to be introduced into the water (by adding new fish or old fish from a winter aquarium) of your pool, release the fish 2 to 3 weeks after the plants are in place. It will take a few weeks for the pond's components to reach a good balance to control algae. Start a fertilization schedule for your plants now. Usually, fertilize your water lilies once a month or so and lotuses about twice as often. The "inject-a-tab" fertilizing instrument works well. The type of soil can influence your fertilization schedule.

SUMMER

In summer, only minimal routine maintenance is needed. The major maintenance is the removal of dead or yellowing pads and spent blossoms from the water lily by cutting the appropriate stems close to the container. This removal of dead pads and blossoms encourages new flower formation. Be sure to keep about 1/3 of the pond's water surface free from vegetation. This allows oxygen into the pool water and contaminating gases to exit the pool water. About every 3 to 4 days (or about twice a week), top off the pool with regular garden hose water. Run this garden hose water into your pool very SLOWLY to minimize temperature changes. Often, one has to add 2 to 3 inches of water height at any one time. If you feed your fish, do so SPARINGLY once every day. If the weather is hot, consider using an aerating pump to keep the oxygen content in your pool's water up. If, by chance, your water lily pads become yellow with poor blossoms, suspect undernourishment. Fertilize all such plants immediately.

FALL

In the fall, the key point is to decide what to do with your plants and fish in the winter. Remember, NEVER allow any of your plant rhizomes to freeze. In

general, use protective pond netting over your pool during the portion of the year when the trees shed their leaves. This helps minimize the accumulation of debris in your pool. Also, make sure all winter equipment is ready and plan on necessary winter precautions.

If you have MILD WINTERS in your area, simply trim excess foliage off of your water lilies and submerge these plant containers to the deepest part of your pool using ropes. No special precautions to your fish or marginal plants need to be taken.

In COLD WINTERS where most of the water does NOT freeze, trim excess foliage off the water lily plants and lower these plant containers to the deepest part of your pool. Be sure that this area is BELOW the line where ice freezing occurs. Be sure that you keep an ice-free area in your pond during the entire winter. If the water surface completely freezes over and stays in this condition, oxygen content in your water will get too low, and the contaminating gas content will accumulate to get too high. This could kill your fish. Your fish will be okay if a decent portion of water has not frozen and if there is an ice-free portion at the water's surface. Marginal plants can be left in your pool as long as their rhizomes don't freeze. For those marginal plants which make outstanding indoor plants, bring them indoors to accent your home. Otherwise, after the first frost turns the foliage brown, cut the stems to about two-thirds of their original height. Never

cut these marginal plant stems below the water line. Some marginal rhizomes (especially cattails) will rot and die if their stems are cut below the water line. If marginal rhizomes will freeze, bring these plants indoors. In cold winters, consider covering your pool to keep it warmer.

In COLD, HARSH WINTERS, special precautions need to be taken. If most of the water is in danger of freezing, consider draining the water from your pool to prevent excess ice pressure against your pool walls due to ice expansion in winter. Then, cover the pool with boards and tarps. If you drain your pool, use this old pool water on your regular gardens as this water is rich in nutrients. Bring your fish and snails indoors into aquariums. For water lilies, first remove excess foliage from your plants. Then, you can do one of three methods. You could bring these plant containers inside a cool area such as a garage or cellar and place these containers into a washtub filled with water for the winter season. Or, one can bring these plant containers into a cool place inside and wrap them with moist blankets. Periodically, check to see if these wrappings are moist. Finally, place a plastic bag around the moistened, wrapped plant container. The third method is to clean the rhizome and place these rhizomes into wet sand in a sealed plastic bag or sealed jar. Marginal plants should be placed indoors. Many marginal plants make excellent house plants in the winter.

Floating plants will disappear in winter as their winter buds fall to the pool's bottom. If possible, place these winter buds in jars of water with a little soil at the jar's bottom. Keep these jars in a lighted, frost-free place like a window sill. In early spring, place these winter buds into warmer water. The other method is to treat floating plants as annuals which need to be restocked each spring.

WINTER

In WARM WINTERS, no special precautions are needed. You have already taken such precautions the previous fall!

In COLD, HARSH WINTERS, consider draining your pool's waters. Then, cover your pool with boards and mark the area to prevent accidents such as falling into the pool. If my advice for the fall is done, the pool would have already been drained and covered to prevent accidents. Your water lilies, marginal plants, and fish would already have been brought indoors to a safe, warmer environment. Hence, no special precautions are needed.

For COLD WINTERS, I am making the assumption that the water lily rhizomes won't freeze. Here, the goal is to keep an ice-free area in your pond throughout the winter. The best portion of the pool to target is a corner area in the southern part of the pool. Hopefully, this portion is the deepest part of your pool. Use of an aerating pump and/or de-icers should be contemplated. If the water does completely freeze over, pour a pot of boiling water SLOWLY onto the ice in one area in order to melt this ice. Never try to crack the ice with a hammer. Such striking of the ice with a hammer may cause the fish to have concussions and die and might cause other damage to your pond. Another way to warm the pool's water is to cover the pool completely with boards and tarps. Cover this completely with either trash bags filled with raked, dry leaves or with a thick layer of straw or hay held in place by evergreen boughs. This acts as insulation to keep the point water from freezing over. Keep this insulation in place with netting. Be sure to mark this area well to prevent accidents. Keep a small hold in the covering that is just over the ice-free portion of your pool. This hold will permit the necessary exchange of gases to occur within the pool's water. The pool's covering will protect against the prevailing northern winds. The fish are kept in the pool and will survive. Place your water lily plant containers in the deepest part of your pool for the winter. If your marginal plants make excellent indoor plants, consider using them to decorate your home in the winter. Otherwise, place the plant containers of your marginal plants in a deep area of the pool. Then, if needed, trim their foliage making sure that some of this foliage remain exposed above the water.

If your pond has the possibility of freezing solid, you should invest in a suitable submergible heater or de-icer. Discuss the purchase with your regular supplier. Photo by Shoichi Suda, courtesy of RINKO magazine.

CONTAINERS, SOIL, DIVISION, STORAGE

This important chapter deals with many topics, including type and size of containers, planting soils, division of rhizomes, and storage of rhizomes over the winter for both water lilies and lotuses.

CONTAINERS

Containers can be of many substances including old wood, wicker, concrete, ceramics, and plastic. I strongly recommend using plastic containers as these are inexpensive, tough, light in weight, easy to drill holes through, and don't absorb water. Use of moveable containers makes it easier to control plant growth, in fertilizing plants, and in the removal of rhizomes either for division or for storing over the winter.

Use solid plastic plant containers. On these containers, drill fairly numerous holes of decent size to allow water to circulate into and out of the container. In addition, place two large holds so that ropes can be inserted in order to raise or lower these containers in the pool. A large drainage hold should be placed at the bottom of the container. This helps in preventing gases from forming that could dislodge the plants. Latticed containers work well.

To a properly ventilated plastic container, I'd recommend using a liner of burlap or fabric mulch. If burlap onion or potato sacks can be found, these make excellent liners. Local nurseries are a source of burlap. Fabric mulch liner, also known as "landscape fabric," is longer lasting than burlap and is available at local nurseries. Liners help allow water circulation through the container in such a way as to prevent soil from spilling into the pool's water. In addition, these liners help in the removal of rhizomes from the container either for rhizome division or for storage of rhizomes over the winter.

It is best to plant a single plant per container. Size of containers should carefully be considered. Larger containers offer two distinct advantages: (1) allow for larger plants with more blooms and (2) provide longer time to occur between rhizome divisions. Keep in mind that both the number of and size of the blooms is in direct proportion to the size of the container. In other words, larger and more numerous flowers are developed by plants in larger containers. Use of large containers will also slow down the frequency of rhizome divisions. Use of bricks and large, smooth stones can be used to obtain a proper depth for your water container. In the specific sections dealing with individual species of water lilies and other plants, container sizes per species of plant will be given.

SOIL AND FERTILIZER

Use of thick, dense, rich topsoil mixed with clay or loam is recommended to grow water lilies, lotuses, and most other of the water plants I will describe. In general, fill the bottom half of the container with this dense soil. Put the necessary fertilizer on the bottom of this soil. Then, place the rhizome into the container with the growing tip towards the center of your container. Follow your supplier's instructions on rhizome placement. Then, work in the rest of your soil by pressing it down with your hands to insure a dense packing of this soil. Be sure to keep one to two inches of the plant container visible. After this, top this soil with at least a one-inch layer of rinsed coarse sand or pea gravel. This top sand or gravel layer prevents the goldfish from uprooting the plants out from the soil and prevents the soil from floating out of the pot to contaminate your pool's water. A flat rock can be placed over the growing tip area to prevent this tip's dislodgment in its first one to two weeks in the water. Plan to use at least a 6-inch layer of soil for most of your water lilies and lotuses in their respective plant containers.

There are many forms of fertilizer available. Stay away from fertilizers using weed or pest chemicals. Follow your supplier's instructions as to how to fertilize your plants. There are time-releasing fertilizing sticks and tablets available. In general, fertilize your water lilies about every 4 to 6 weeks. If your water lilies display a significant number of yellowing pads along with poor blooms, suspect undernourishment. Use good fertilizer immediately when undernourishment is suspected.

When your containers are ready for the pool, place the container near the pool and soak it once or twice with water. By using ropes, SLOWLY immerse these containers into your pool, usually at a slant. This will allow plant-dislodging gases to escape without harming your plants. This procedure will minimize chances of churning or clouding your pool water. Use of ropes will help save your back when lowering or raising your plant containers.

In general, place hardy water lily rhizomes at a 45° angle when placing them into the soil. Certain Marliac varieties of hardies use a vertical placement of rhizomes. Usually, tropical water lily rhizome placement is in the vertical position. Typically, the lotus placement is in the horizontal fashion. The above are general guidelines for rhizome placement. However, it is best to follow the specific instructions of your water lily or lotus supplier on rhizome placement.

RHIZOME STORAGE

If you live in warm climates, you can sink water lily plant containers to the bottom of your pool. Special care may be needed for tropical water lily rhizomes. If the weather is very cold, bring these plant containers indoors and place them into the water of a filled wash tub. The two general rhizome storage methods outside of being placed into a water container will now be discussed.

In the first storage technique, either no rhizome division will be done at all or will be performed in the spring. In this method, pull your plant containers out of your pool water and let them drain for several hours. Then, wrap each container with a wet burlap or blanket covering. Place each burlap or blanket wrapped container into a plastic bag and seal this plastic bag with a bag tie. This plastic bag helps to insure keeping the moisture in. Place these properly sealed containers in a cool place like a basement or garage where temperatures are about 40 to 55° F (or 4.0° to 12.5° C) all winter. Be sure to check on the wetness of both the soil and the burlap or blanket covering every two to three weeks. If needed, add appropriate wetness to both the soil and the burlap or blanket covering the container. Be sure to tie the plastic bag every time you check on the moisture.

The second method involves thoroughly washing the soil from a good rhizome and then place this rhizome in wet sand. To obtain the proper sand moisture consistency, place sand in a perforated plant container and saturate this container thoroughly with water. Let this container drain for about 4 to 5 hours. Place more than enough of this wet sand to thoroughly surround the rhizome in a zipper-locked plastic bag. Be sure that you have a proper identifying label for the rhizome stored in each bag. Use only one rhizome per bag and store these bags in a cool place like a basement. Check every 2 weeks or so to see if the sand is damp. Add water if needed. Some people use sealed jars stored in bedrooms to store rhizomes. Check to see that the sand is moist periodically, this alternative storage method works well.

RHIZOME DIVISION

In general, rhizomes should be hard in consistency like a new potato or be just a little spongier and have a fresh scent like soil. If the rhizome is gelatinous looking or is foul smelling, throw it away.

In general, for hardy water lily and lotus rhizomes, wash them thoroughly before division. Look for the "eyes" (buds or growing tips). Then, simply cut the rhizomes into about 4 to 5 inch chunks with each chunk having at least one "eye." Use a heavily serrated knife or a hacksaw in a "sawing" manner to cut the rhizomes into appropriate chunks. Do NOT chop at the rhizomes. After all this, dress each cut end in either charcoal or sulfur. Perform rhizome division on hardy water lilies and lotuses whenever indicated during the fall or spring. If this division of rhizomes is performed in the fall, store this chunk in an appropriate manner for the winter. If the rhizome division is done in the spring, place this chunk into a suitable plant container and then place this plant container into your pool.

In colder climates, many treat tropical water lilies as annuals. In other words, they order new rhizomes every year. Try to save appropriate rhizomes over the winter. Rhizome division for tropical water lilies is done in the fall. For tropical water lilies, simply clean the rhizome thoroughly and let dry.

Separate the grape-to walnut-sized eyes from the rhizome and place these eyes into warm water for one to two days. Discard any of the eyes that float. Keep only the viable eyes that sink. For these viable eyes, store them in wet sand in either a zipper-locked plastic bag or sealed jar. This method for storing tropical eyes often works but is not foolproof. There is some trouble in raising tropical rhizomes to a proper size worth planting. For tropical rhizomes, I'd recommend storing them in a relatively warm place over the winter. A proper identifying label should be with each tropical water lily rhizome.

PLANTING SEASON

HARDY WATER LILIES

As the name indicates, the hardy water type of water lily is the most tolerant of weather and is the easiest to grow especially in cool climates. Typically, the blooms float directly on the water's surface. These blooms, which are often cup or bowl shaped, often display white, yellow, pink, orange, or red colors. These flowers are day bloomers which last from three to five days. If overcrowding conditions exist, the blooms can rise above the water's surface. Hardies can survive well in cold weather and can remain outdoors in the winter if the pool is deep enough.

The hardy water lilies can generally be planted by early spring when the water temperatures reach 50° F (or 10° C) or more. Usually, this is from the end of March to the end of April. Use bricks or large smooth stones to set a proper water depth of about 4 inches over the top of the planting container. As the

PLANTING A WATER LILY
Photos by Anita Nelson

Left: Use pots without drainage holes. Use clay loam soil. Fill pot 1/3 full. Plant lily in at least 10 quarts of soil. Use larger pots for larger lilies. **Center:** Fertilize with a slow-release tablet fertilizer. **Right:** Use one fertilizer tablet for each 5 quarts of soil.

Top left: Pound the soil with your fist. This compacts the soil and rids it of trapped pockets of air. Top center: Planting a hardy lily requires that you fill the pot up to 2 inches from the rim. Make a shallow trench from side to center. Lay the lily rhizome in with the growth tip in the center. Cover with soil and pound with your fist. If planting a tropical lily, make a cone of the soil in the center of the pot. Place the rhizome over the center of the cone. Spread the roots around the cone. Fill it gradually with soil and then pound out the trapped air. Top right: Add one inch of pea gravel to the top. This will prevent the fish from uprooting the plants. Bottom left: Fill with water. Bottom center: If you're not going to put in the water lily right away, cover it with very wet newspaper. Botttom right: Lower the pot slowly into the pond. The escaping air bubbles could uproot the plant. Should this happen, simply push the lily back into the soil.

Spread the leaves out.

pads adjust to this water, depth, gradually lower the plant container in like fashion in 2 to 3 inch increments until about a 12-inch water depth layer exists over your plant container. If, however, your pool is in a shady area, you may want to use a 6-to 8-inch water depth layer over your plant container as your final water depth level.

TROPICAL WATER LILIES

As the name indicates, tropical water lilies grow best in warm climates. These plants are larger and showier than the hardy water lilies. Typically, the tropical blooms are held high over the water's surface and are relatively flat in shape. Tropical blooms display a wider range of colors than hardies by including the exotic hues of blues and purples in addition to the usual hardy range of colors.

The tropical blossoms are classified as either day blooming or as night blooming varieties. These blossoms can last up to 5 days. The pads are often very beautiful and large. Place the tropical water lilies into your pool waters only after your pool waters reach temperatures of 65 to 70° F (or 18 to 21° C). Tropical water lilies often need twice as much water surface space as hardy water lilies.

Many treat tropical water lilies as annuals due to problems in storage of, or division of, their rhizomes. Wait until pool waters have reached a minimum of 70° F (or 21° C). Hence, planting time generally runs from May to June depending on where you live. If you have stored these rhizomes or if you have divided them, check in early spring to see if the eyes of the rhizomes have sprouted. If not, place the eyes into warm water on a sunny window sill until the eye sprouts. Then, place these sprouted eyes into 5-inch pots with heavy garden soil and a top layer of gravel. Be sure to identify each pot as to the species of eye that it contains. Set these pots into a large aquarium with heated water of at least 70° F (or 21° C) and at least 3 inch water depth layer over these pots. Keep this water at least 70° F (or 21° C) at all times. Keep these plants in this aquarium for about 2 to 6 weeks when the new pads begin to show. When your outside pool's water temperatures reach 70° F (or 21° C) and stays at this temperature as a minimum temperature, you can move your tropical water lily from the aquarium to your outside pool. When you do so, be sure

to use a larger-sized plant container (generally, a 13" by 9" size) and follow the general instructions given for hardy water lilies as to proper water depths.

LOTUSES

Lotuses are exotic, large, graceful plants displaying exquisite blooms in white, cream, yellow, pink, and red colors. These blossoms can measure 10 to 12 inches in diameter. The large, green, umbrella-shaped pads can measure 2 feet across! The key distinguishing feature is the golden-colored seed pod shaped like a faucet's "nozzle." Seeds from this pod can remain viable for about 2,000 years. For the American Yellow Lotus (N*elumbo lutea*), I have measured blooms rising over 4 feet out of the water and pads towering over 3 feet out of the water. The *Nelumbo nucifera* is the sacred pink lotus of Asia. From this pink sacred lotus, many

Close up showing a Yellow American Lotus. Photo by the author.

Above left: Sometimes the pond is deeper than where the lily originally came from and the leaves may be submerged. Don't worry...the leaves will grow to the surface in a day or so (depending upon the temperature of the water). Above right: This is the pond before pruning the lily leaves. Each leaf (or pad) begins to turn yellow after it is four weeks old. You can remove it by pinching it off at the base of the plant. If the water is deep this isn't always easy! Below left: *Nymphaea madame*—the blossom floats directly on the water's surface. Photo by the author. Below right: The same pond after pruning.

Below right: Fertilize with slow-release tablets every 2-4 weeks during the growing season. The hotter the water, the faster the plants grow and the more fertilizer will be needed. Below left: A Sandwich-man Caterpillar in the center of the leaf sandwiches himself between the leaves. Remove it by hand and drop it into the water for the fish to eat.

 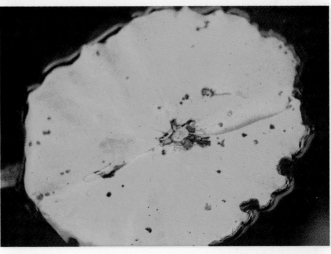

hybrids called cultivars are now being developed.

In early spring, lotuses can be planted when pool waters are in the upper 40's° F (or about 8 to 10° C) - about at the same time when the hardy water lilies are planted. For regular sized lotuses, use large plant containers measuring 16 inches in diameter by 7 inches in height or larger. Some miniature lotuses can be planted in 10 inch pots. Follow the instructions given for the hardy water lilies on setting proper water depth levels for your lotuses.

For lotuses, it is possible to use the seeds from a fully matured brown seed pod. These seeds can remain viable for 2,000 years! Raising lotuses from seeds, however, is beyond the scope of this book.

Above: *Nymphaea caerulea*, the Blue Lotus of Ancient Egypt, also known as the Blue Lotus of the Nile. The photo shows a bud and an opening flower. Photo by the author.

VICTORIAS

In 1801, Europeans first discovered the Victoria plant growing in the Amazon basin of South America. In the late 1830's, John Lindley named this plant Victoria regia in honor of the young queen of England, Victoria. Today, the scientific name for Victoria regia is Victoria amazonica. The Longwood Gardens in Pennsylvania developed the Victoria longwood cultivar which is a cross between Victoria amazonica and Victoria cruziana. This Victoria plant is by far the most spectacular as its pads can grow 6 to 8 feet in diameter and its blooms can measure 14 inches across! These pads can support weights of 100 to 200 pounds. In San Angelo, Texas, Mr. Ken Landon's Victoria pads average over 6 feet in diameter with rims about 4 to 5 inches tall! This spectacular plant is beyond the scope of this book due to its immense size. A single Victoria plant can reach 25 to 30 feet in diameter.

WATER DEPTH

Typically, both hardy and tropical water lilies usually require 6 to 18 inches of water over the soil. I have given 12 inches as the water depth as a general rule of thumb for both water lilies and lotuses. For shaded pool areas, less water depth may be needed. Some lotuses may require shallower water depths of about 4 to 8 inches.

Left: *Victoria longwood* has huge pads 6 to 8 feet across. This hybrid species resulted from crossing *Victoria amazonica* with *Victoria cruziana*. Photo by the author.

Above left: Ready, get set, GO! The pots are filled with clay loam. Cinder blocks are used to raise the water lilies to their proper depth of 18-24 inches in a 36-inch deep pond. Above left: Soon after planting the lilies will triple in size.

Above left: The same view three weeks later. Above right: Adding bog plants to the pond...getting the planting containers ready. Below left: Placing the plants in the pond. Below right: Immediately after planting.

WATER LILIES AND LOTUSES

In this chapter, I will give general information on hardy water lilies, tropical water lilies, and the true lotus. In addition, I will describe good examples of different species in each category that even a beginner can easily grow. In some cases, I have a photograph of the species described.

For beginners, I'd strongly recommend starting with the hardy type of water lily as these are the easiest to grow - especially in cooler climates. Some of the tropical water lilies are fairly easy to grow. If one lives in a hot and humid climate, a tropical water lily could be the water lily of choice. The lotuses should be the last category that a beginner should try.

My list only describes some of the best water lily and lotus species available for a beginner to incorporate into his or her water garden. There are other excellent water lily and lotus species for a beginner to start with. If a local nursery or a friend has a beautiful water lily that is a prolific bloomer over a long season, then a beginner could choose to start with this specific water lily as it seems to be dependable for that water gardener's specific climate. If doing so, then, I would get any helpful hints that the local nursery or friend has to give you. Again, in general, the best advice is to start with a known, dependable species such as those described in this chapter.

HARDY WATER LILIES

As the name indicates, the hardy type of water lily is the easiest type to grow especially in cooler climates. Typically, the blooms float directly on the water's surface. These blossoms often display a cut or bowl shape in exotic whites, yellows, pinks, and reds. The hardy blooms are only the day blooming type. Hardies can survive well in cold weather and remain outdoors in the pool if that pool is deep enough. For a beginner to start, I'd strongly recommend trying dependable and proven species of hardy water lilies. In general, hardy water lilies do much better than tropical water lilies in cooler climates. The hardy blooms typically last for 3 days or more in duration.

RECOMMENDED HARDY WATER LILIES

Helvola

HELVOLA (*Nymphaea helvola*) - also known an "pigmy yellow." A true miniature, yellow hardy water lily. It has small 2-inch blooms, a pad spread of 1 to 1.5 square feet, is free blooming, and adapts very well to shade. IDEAL FOR TUBS AND KETTLES. It might be best to keep the Holvola away from regular-sized water lilies as these may tend to crowd out the Helvola.

Chromatella

CHROMATELLA (*Nymphaea chromatella*) - also known as "golden cup." It

Nymphaea chromatella. **Photo by the author.**

has rich canary yellow blossoms, can withstand cold weather, adapts fairly well to shade, and is an early bloomer with a long blooming season. IDEAL FOR TUBS AND KETTLES. Can grow in any sized pool. Pad spread is usually 4 to 12 square feet. Has 4 to 5 1/2 inch flowers.

Fabiola

FABIOLA (*Nymphaea fabiola* or *Nymphaea* pink beauty) - also known as "pink

Nymphaea fabiola also known as *Nymphaea Pink Beauty*. **Photo by the author.**

beauty." It is a prolific bloomer favoring full sun. IDEAL FOR TUBS AND KETTLES. Can grow in any sized pool. Pad spread is

A grouping of *Nymphaea hermine*. Photo by the author.

usually 4 to 12 square feet. To some, newer scientific names if *Nymphaea luciana.*. Has 6 inch flowers.

Hermine

HERMINE (*Nymphaea hermine*) - A small pure white hardy water lily. It is free blooming over a long blooming season, adapts fairly well to shade, and has bright green pads. IDEAL FOR TUBS AND KETTLES. Can grow in any sized pool. Pad spread is usually 4 to 12 feet. A Marliac hybrid. Has 5 inch flowers.

Gloriosa

GLORIOSA (N*ymphaea gloriosa*)) - A carmine rose colored hardy water lily species with blossoms 5 to 6 inches across. Adapts well to shade. IDEAL FOR TUBS AND KETTLES. Can grow in any sized pool. Has 5 inch flowers.

Aurora

AURORA (*Nymphaea aurora*) - A changing-colored water lily in which the colors range from yellow to orange to

Nymphaea gloriosa. Photo by the author.

deep red. IDEAL FOR TUBS AND KETTLES. Can grow in any sized pool. Has 4 to 4 1/2 inch flowers.

Texas dawn

TEXAS DAWN (*Nymphaea*

Nymphaea Texas Dawn developed by Ken Landon. Photo by the author.

texas galore dawn) - An exciting rich yellow cultivar developed by Ken Landon of San Angelo. It is a prolific bloomer with a long blooming season. Adapts fairly well to shade and is very fragrant. GROWS WELL IN TUBS ESPECIALLY IN WARMER CLIMATES. Grows well in any

Nymphaea aurora. Photo by the author.

Nymphaea James Brydon **represented by an open flower and two buds. Photo by the author.**

sized pool. Blooms often measure 6 to 8 inches in diameter. Pad spread usually is 9 to 18 square feet.

James Brydon

JAMES BRYDON (*Nymphaea james brydon*) - A pinkish to crimson red water lily with blooms 5 inches across. Adapts fairly well to shade, is very fragrant, works well in temperate climates, and is prolific in blooming. Suitable for most

Nymphaea masaniello. **Photo by the author.**

sizes of pools. Some people grow this species in kettles. Pad spread is usually 6 to 12 square feet.

Masaniello

MASANIELLO (*Nymphaea masaniello*) - A rose-pink hardy water lily with 5 inch blooms. Is fragrant, easy for beginners to grow in most sizes of pools, and adapts fairly well to shade. Pad spread is usually 6 to 12 square feet.

Peter Slocum

PETER SLOCUM (*Nymphaea peter slocum*) - A spectacular and beautiful rich pink double flower. It very fragrant, favors direct sun, has a long blooming season, and displays cup shaped blooms. Does well in most sized pools. Pad spread usually is 9 to 18 square feet. Has 6 to 7 inch flowers.

Arc en ciel

ARC EN CIEL (*Nymphaea arc en ciel*) - A variable colored (usually either white or pink) water lily with mottled pads. Favors direct sun. Excellent choice for medium to larger pools. Pad spread usually is 9 to 18 square feet. In French, arc-en-ciel means the "arch in the sky" or a rainbow! Has 5 to 6 inch flowers.

Nymphaea Peter Slocum, **a hardy. Photo by Anita Nelson.**

Nymphaea Arc en Ciel. **Photo by Anita Nelson.**

HARDY WATER LILY CONTAINER SIZES

Helvola .... 1 Quart .... 4" x 4"

Helvola .... 1 Gallon .... 8" x 5 1/2"
Small Hardies

Chromatella .... 1 Gallon .... 8" x 5 1/2"
Fabiola .... 2 Gallon .... 8" x 8"
Hermine
Gloriosa
Aurora

Small Hardies .... 2 Gallon .... 8" x 8"
Standard Hardies .... 10" x 8"

Texas Dawn.. 10" x 8"
 .... 4 Gallon .... 13" x 9"
Large Hardies .... 4 Gallon .... 13" x9"
All Other Listed Species

NOTE: For the above, the 13" x 9" container is essentially the same size as a 12 $^5/_8$" x 9 $^1/_{16}$" container. These containers are interchangeable. These are the minimal recommended container sizes for the above hardy water lilies. Larger-sized containers offer these two distinct advantages: (1) larger plants with more blooms, and (2) fewer rhizome divisions.

Nymphaea Arc en Ciel. Photo by the author.

Nymphaea virginalis. Photo by the author.

A group of three flowers of *Nymphaea virginalis*. Photo by the author.

A pond full of hardy water lilies.
Photo by Anita Nelson.

Virginalis

VIRGINALIS (**Nymphaea virginalis**) - A pure white water lily with large blooms. Favors direct sun, has a long blooming season, and displays cup shaped blossoms. Does well in most sized pools. Pad spread usually is from 9 to 18 square feet. Has 5 inch flowers.

TROPICAL WATER LILIES

As the name indicates, tropical water lilies are best grown in warm climates. These plants are larger and showier than the hardy water lilies. Typically, tropical blooms are held high over the water's surface and are relatively flat in shape. Tropical flowers display a wider range of colors than hardies by including exotic blues and purples as well as the usual hardy water lily range of colors. The blooms are classified as night or day blooming varieties.. To grow tropical water lilies, the pool's water must be at least 65° to 70° F (or about 18° to 21° C). Tropical water lilies thrive in warm climates.

Nymphaea colorata, also known as the Wisteria Blue day blooming tropical water lily. Photo by Anita Nelson.

Dauben

DAUBEN (**Nymphaea daubeniana**) - A great pastel blue day blooming tropical water lily. Performs extremely well in shade, is a prolific bloomer, takes well to some cold weather, has small blooms, and adapts well to small containers. Is a hybrid from the ancient Egyptian blue "lotus," **Nymphaea caerulea**. This is the best water lily for poorly lit areas. IDEAL FOR TUBS AND KETTLES. Also excellent for small pools. Pad spread usually is from 4 to 12 square feet. Has 4 to 6 inch flowers.

Nymphaea daubeniana, a blue day blooming tropical water lily. Photo by Anita Nelson.

Colorata

COLORATA (*Nymphaea colorata*) - A Williamsburg or wisteria blue (a deeper blue) colored day blooming tropical water lily. It is a prolific bloomer and adapts fairly well to shade. IDEAL FOR TUBS AND KETTLES. Pad spread is usually only 1 to 6 square feet. Has 5 inch flowers.

Panama pacific

PANAMA PACIFIC (*Nymphaea panama pacific*) - A rich violet colored day blooming tropical water lily. It is a good bloomer, is fragrant, adapts fairly well to shade. IDEAL FOR TUBS AND KETTLES. Adapts well to any sized pool. Pad spread usually is 4 to 18 square feet. Has 4 1/2 to 6 inch flowers.

Madame ganna walska

MADAME GANNA WALSKA (*Nymphaea madame ganna walska*) - An exotic violet-pink colored day blooming tropical water lily. It is easy to grow, adapts fairly well to shade, and is a prolific bloomer. IDEAL FOR TUBS

Nymphaea St. Louis Gold. **Photo by the author.**

Above left: *Nymphaea Madame Ganna Walska*, **a day blooming tropical water lily. Photo by the author. Above right:** *Nymphaea Madame Ganna Walska*, **at the Missouri Botanical Gardens in St. Louis, Missouri. Photo by the author. Below: St. Louis Gold, a day blooming tropical water lily. Photo by Anita Nelson.**

AND KETTLES. Pad spread is usually from 4 to 12 square feet.

St. Louis gold
ST. LOUIS GOLD (***Nymphaea st. louis gold***) - An exquisite golden colored day blooming tropical water lily. In many ways, this is one of the best of the tropical water lilies. This species is excellent for beginners to grow and has blooms all season long. IDEAL FOR TUBS AND KETTLES. Adapts well to all sizes of pools. Has 5 to 6 inch flowers.

General pershing
GENERAL PERSHING (***Nymphaea general pershing***) - A large, vigorous orchid-pink colored day blooming tropical water lily. Has large 8 to 10 inch blooms, stays open during the day longer than most water lilies, and adapts well in small to large pools. Adapts fairly well to shade and has a long blooming season. Pad spread is usually 9 to 18 square feet.

Blue beauty
BLUE BEAUTY (***Nmyphaea blue beauty***) - Also know as

Above: *Nymphaea General Pershing* in a three flower portrait. Photo by the author. Left: *Nymphaea General Pershing* is a large day blooming tropical. Photo by the author.

TROPICAL WATER LILY CONTAINER SIZE

Colorata .... 2 Gallon .... 8" x 8"
.... 10" x 8"

Tropical Water Lilies4 Gallon .... 13" x 9"
(in general)

NOTE: The 13" x 9" and the 12 5/8" x 9 1/16" containers are interchangeable. These are the minimal container sizes for tropical water lilies. Larger sized containers offer two distinctadvantages! (1) larger plants with more blooms and (2) fewer rhizome divisions.

Nymphaea Pennsylvania or as "Pennsylvania." Is a sky blue colored day blooming tropical water lily. It is a prolific bloomer, has magnificent 10 inch blossoms. Is a hybrid developed from the ancient Egyptian blue "lotus," Nymphaea caerulea. Favors full sun and adapts well to most pool sizes. Pad spread usually is from 9 to 18 square feet.

LOTUSES

Lotuses are exotic, large, graceful plants displaying exotic blossoms in white, cream, yellow, pink, and red colors. The blossoms can measure 10 to 12 inches in diameter while the umbrella shaped pads can measure 2 feet across! The key distinguishing feature is the golden colored seed pod shaped like a faucet's "nozzle." In the young blossom, the seed pod is golden. As this blossom matures, the seed pod starts to turn green. After the blossom dies, this seed pod will turn entirely green and finally turn to a brown color. Lotus seeds from the seed pod can remain viable for about 2,000 years. For the American Yellow Lotus, *Nelumbo lutea*, I have measured blooms rising over 4 feet out of the water with pads towering over 3 feet above the water's surface! The *Nelumbo nucifera* is the sacred lotus of Asia. From this pink sacred lotus, many hybrids are now being developed.

For growing lotuses, a medium to larger pool is recommended. However, some lotuses can be grown in tubs and kettles. In some cases, a whiskey half-barrel was used

Above: *Nymphaea caerulea*, the Blue Lotus of Ancient Egypt. Photo by the author. Below: *Nymphaea lotus* variety *dentata*, the White Lotus of Ancient Egypt. Photo by the author

Nelumbo lutea, the American yellow lotus. In this portrait are two blossoms, an opening flower from a bud, a bud, seed pods and many pads. A blossom can measure 11 inches in diameter while a pad can be 2 feet across. Photo by the author.

Above: *Nymphaea lotus* variety *dentata*, the White Lotus of Ancient Egypt. Below: *Nelumbo lutea*, the American yellow lotus, as seen in Lake Manawa State Park, Council Bluffs, Iowa. Photo by the author.

as both the container and the tub pool for the lotus.

Chawan basu

CHAWAN BASU (**N***elumbo* ***nucifera*** "chawan basu") - has white to cream colored blooms with pink edges. Does well in tubs and kettles in the full sun. This plant grows about 1.5 to 4 feet tall. Chawan basu translates as "rice bowl." Has 5 to 9 inch blooms.

Momo botan

MOMO BOTAN (***Nelumbo nucifera*** "momo botan") - has deep rose-red double flowers resembling peonies. In fact, in Japanese, "momo botan" means "like a double peony!" This plant grows 1.5 to 4 feet tall and has pads measuring 12 to 18 inches across. Does well in tubs and kettles in the full sun. Has 5 to 6 inch blooms.

Tulip lotus or Shirokunshi

TULIP LOTUS or SHIROKUNSHI (***Nelumbo nucifera*** "shirokunshi") - Also called the "Shirokunshi" lotus. Has pure white blossoms and grows to 1.5 to 2 feet tall. Does well in tubs and kettles. Has 7 to 8 inch blooms.

Baby doll

BABY DOLL (a ***Nelumbo nucifera*** variety) - has white blossoms measuring 4 to 5 inches across. Grows 1.5 to 2 feet tall. Does well in tubs and kettles. Has 4 to 6 inch flowers.

OTHER TUB AND KETTLE LOTUSES

Other varieties of lotuses that grow well in tubs

include: Charles Thomas (pink-lavender) and Angel Wings (white). These are also **Nelumbo nucifera** varieties.

Sacred pink lotus

SACRED PINK LOTUS (**Nelumbo nucifera**) - Also called Improved Egyptian Pink, Improved Egyptian Lotus, Hindu Lotus. Other scientific names include: **Nelumbium speciosum** and **Nelumbo nucifera speciosum**. This is a very large plant with pink or red blossoms measuring up to 12 inches across and has large inverted umbrella-shaped pads. Is a very durable plant in nature with seeds remaining viable for about 2,000 years. Some people have grown this species in tubs and kettles. Many hybrids have been developed from this sacred lotus of Asia. If growing this lotus, I would recommend using a medium to large pool. Has pads measuring up to 3 feet across.

American yellow lotus

AMERICAN YELLOW LOTUS (**Nelumbo lutea**) - Also called a "water chinaquin." Has large, vivid lemon-yellow colored blossoms measuring up to 11 inches in diameter which can rise over 4 feet out of the water. The large, green, umbrella-shaped pads which can measure 2 feet in diameter can tower over 3 feet out of the water. This is an extremely durable plant. This lotus's territory ranges from New England to Texas. I have seen this lotus in both Iowa and Texas. If growing this plant, I would recommend using a medium to large pool.

LOTUS CONTAINER SIZES

Small or tub lotuses .... 13" x 9"
(or 12 5/8" x 9 1/16")

Regular lotuses .... 16" x 7-9"
(or 23" x 7-10")

NOTE: Some use a whiskey half barrel as both the container and tub pool for small lotuses.

Nelumbo lutea, the American yellow lotus, showing an open blossom containing the seed pod. Photographed at Lake Manawa State Park by the author.

Above: Growing next to the lily is *Elodea canadensis*, a very common aquarium plant available at most aquarium stores. Photo by the author. Below: Parrot Feather, *Myriophyllum aquaticum*, growing out of the water. This is a common aquatic, submerged plant. It is available at most aquarium stores. Photo by the author.

OTHER PLANTS

In general, other plants consist of submerged, floating, and marginal plants. Submerged plants are called oxygenating plants because their underwater leaves supply oxygen to the pool's water. Submerged plants also absorb other impurities and carbon dioxide from the water. As its name indicates, floating plants simply float on the water's surface. These plants are great water purifiers as they remove many contaminants from the water. Marginal plants are shallow water plants that provide finishing touches to a delightful water garden pool.

SUBMERGED PLANTS

Submerged plants are also known as oxygenating plants because their underwater green leaves produce oxygen during photosynthesis for the fish in your pool. These plants absorb carbon dioxide from fish, waste material, and decaying matter. Submerged plants also absorb some impurities from the water. These two actions help starve out algae. Another name for submerged plants is "bunched" plants because they are usually supplied in a few stems (usually 6 stems) per bunch. These submerged plant's green leaves serve as a foliage food for the fish. Use of plastic meshed domes for submerged plants are recommended to prevent the fish from overeating these plants. One can develop new submerged plants by taking 5 to 6 inch cuttings from the main plant.

In general, use a rich clay type of soil to plant your submerged plants and be sure to top this soil off with a 3/4 to 1 inch layer of coarse sand or pea gravel. This top layer prevents your fish from uprooting these plants. As submerged plants usually arrive with lead weights, be sure to plant the stems in such a manner that the lead weights are totally into the soil without contacting the water. Otherwise, if this lead contacts the water directly, the submerged plant stems will rot at the point of the lead contacting water. These lead weights are added to prevent these plants from floating upwards in the water. Their underwater stems and leaves provide fish with spawning grounds.

Elodea
ELODEA (**Elodea canadensis** or **Egeria densa**) - Also known as Anacharis or Canadian pondweed. It competes with algae for the same mineral salts and carbon dioxide. If enough of this plant is used, the water should be crystal clear most of the growing season. It provides a good supply of oxygen to the water. Plant in at least 12 inches of water.

Parrot feather
PARROT FEATHER (**Myriophyllum aquaticum**) - Adapts well to full sun and shade. It is a creeper in the pool with its beautiful tufted heads rising just a few inches above the water. From South America. It provides spawning

Cabomba caroliniana **is a very common plant for aquarium use. It is very valuable in water gardens, too.**

area for the fish, is green in color, and is very vigorous. Plant in at least 12 inches of water.

Cabomba
CABOMBA (**Cabomba caroliniana**) - is another submerged plant supplying oxygen to your pool. It is also known as water milfoil.

FLOATING PLANTS
Floating plants are great plants that naturally purify the water from many contaminants. In fact, some of our reclamation centers use these floating plants to purify some of their water. These plants often do the same work as six submerged plants. When discarding floating plants, use them in your mulches. Never flush floating plants down the toilet. Water hyacinth and water lettuce are the two major floating plants.

Water lettuce
WATER LETTUCE (**Pistia stratiotes**) - is a first rate water clearer and purifier. It has a lettuce-like leafy "rosette" appearance. Simply drop this plant into your water at 69° F or above (or

Water Lettuce, *Pistia stratiotes*. **Photo by the author.**

about 20.5° C). Has extensive root system that cleans water of many impurities. Does well in full sun and fairly well in shade. Has insignificant flowers. Is smaller than water hyacinth. Be careful of laws that could protect this plant. It competes against algae for nutrients.

Water hyacinth
WATER HYACINTH (**Eichhornia crassipes**) - A first rate water clearer and purifier. Was named after the Prussian minister of education, Mr. Eichhorn. It has long black roots trailing into the water, which clear the water of many impurities. Has nice lavender-colored flowers. Will form "turions" (or buds) before winter. These buds will form new plants in the following spring. Simply toss these buds into the water

SUBMERGED PLANT CONTAINER SIZES		
Submerged plants	1 Gallon	8" x 5 1/2"
Submerged plants	1 Gallon	8" x 8"

Above: Fertilizers designed for use with potted plants in garden ponds are available at pet shops and aquatic garden centers. The best such fertilizers are kept low in phosphate content to discourage the growth of algae. Photo courtesy of Jungle Laboratories Corporation. Below: Papyrus, *Cyperus papyrus*. Photo by the author.

when its temperature is relatively warm. This plant has a history of cloggiing waterways and is often protected by federal and state laws. This plant, which can grow to a fairly large size, helps to clear the water of algae. If you have too many water hyacinths in your pool, place them into a compost. Never flush this plant down a toilet. Some reclamation centers use water hyacinths to provide nature's way of purifying water.

FLOATING PLANT CONTAINER SIZES

As these plants float in your water garden pool, NO plant containers are used.

MARGINAL PLANTS

Marginal plants are shallow water plants that add height and texture to a water garden pool. Marginal plants are also called bog plants, aquatic plants, aquatic bog plants, shallow water plants, and accent plants. These marginal plants are shallow water plants that accent your pool by providing a nice finishing touch. Some of these plants make terrific house plants. Flowering marginal plants include irises, cannas, thalias, and some water hibiscus.

When planting marginal plants, use rich clay soil and top this with a 3/4 to 1 inch layer of coarse sand or pea gravel. This top layer of sand or gravel prevents the soil from contaminating the water. Some people use river rock gravel as their top layer.

Papyrus

PAPYRUS (*Cyperus papyrus*) - Also known as giant papyrus, Egyptian paper plant, and paper reed. It favors full sun, tolerates some shade, and prefers 0 to 6 inches of water over it. Grows six to ten feet tall. Usually, if possible, winter this plant indoors in a sunny room. Then, reset it outdoors in the following spring. The umbel "mop-heads" will dip into the water in the fall, which can lead to new plants. Papyrus was the sacred plant of Northern Egypt of the Nile Delta region in the era of Ramses II (about 1250 BC). In ancient times, papyrus grew to 15 feet in height.

Above: Papyrus and Water Hyacinth at the Gabelhouse's pond in Lincoln, Nebraska. Photo by the author. Below left: Dwarf Papyrus, *Cyperus haspans*. Photo by the author. Below right: Dwarf Papyrus, *Cyperus haspans*. Photo by the author.

Dwarf Papyrus

DWARF PAPYRUS (*Cyperus haspans*) - one book has the scientific names as *Cyperus isocladus*. This small, delightful plant favors both full sun and shade equally well, grows 24 to 30 inches tall, makes an ideal indoor house plant, and favors 0 to 6 inches of water over it. It is outstanding in tubs and kettles.

Umbrella palm

UMBRELLA PALM (*Cyperus alternifolius*) - Usually, this excellent accent plant grows 2 to 4 feet tall, favors both full sun and shade equally well, makes an outstanding indoor house plant, and favors 0 to 6 inches of water over it. Does well in tubs and kettles. Has

Umbrella Palm, *Cyperus alternifolius*. Photo by the author.

Umbrella Palm, *Cyperus alternifolius*. Photo by the author.

a dwarf version called "gracilis" which grows to 2 feet. Umbrella palms provide an exciting look to almost any location.

Common cattail

COMMON CATTAIL (*Typha latifolia*) - This plant can grow to 7 or 8 feet in height to make a striking accent plant for medium to large pools. It favors full sun and partial sun and does well with 0 to 12 inches of water over it. It has beautiful brown, velvety, chocolate colored flowers resembling the shape of a cat's tail! Leave the "lifeless" stems in place in the winter as these stems supply oxygen to the roots. If these stems are <u>not</u> left in place, the cattails will die. This goes for any variety of cattail.

Dwarf cattail

DWARF CATTAIL (*Typha minima*) - this plant grows to

Above: Common Cattail, *Typha latifolia*. Photo by the author. Below: Common Cattail flower. Photo by the author.

2 feet tall. It is outstanding in tubs and kettles, favors full sun and partial sun, and prefers 0 to 2 inches of water over it.

Graceful cattail

GRACEFUL CATTAIL (*Typha angustifolia*) - This plant can grow to 4 feet tall, favors full sun and partial sun, and prefers 0 to 12 inches of water over it. Can grow in tubs and kettles.

Arrowhead

ARROWHEAD (*Sagittaria latifoolia*) - This plant grows 1 to 3 feet tall, gets its name for its unusually shaped leaf, favors full sun and partial sun, and prefers 0 to 6 inches of water over it. It is easy to grow. Smaller arrowheads are excellent for tubs and kettles.

Arrowhead, *Sagittaria latifolia*. Photo by the author.

Sagittaria

SAGITTARIA - A narrow leafed plant which grows 24 inches tall. It favors both full sun and shade equally well and prefers 0 to 12 inches of water over it. This plant works well in tubs and kettles.

Dwarf Sag, *Sagittaria subulata*. Photo by the author.

Typha angustifolia, the cattail. Photo by Anita Nelson.

Pickerel Weed, *Pondeteria cordata* is the green plant. The red plant is *Lobelia cardinalis.* Photo by the author.

Pickerel rush

PICKEREL RUSH (***Pondeteria cordata***) - Its common name is "wampee." This plant is named after the Italian botanist, Giulio Pondeteria. This plant favors heavy and loamy (clay) soil, prefers full sun, and has purple to violet colored flowers. It is a very durable plant. Other varieties of this plant have white or blue flowers.

Horsetail rush

HORSETAIL RUSH (***Equisetum hyemele***) - This plant has green jointed stems with a small "cone" on top. It grows to 2 to 3 feet in height. Is a durable plant. Also known as the scouring rush.

Above: Pickerel Weed flower, *Pondeteria cordata.* Photo by the author. Below: Horsetail Rush, also known as Scouring Rush, *Equisetum hyemele.* Photo by the author.

Green Taro, *Colocasia esculente.* This variety has a purple stem. Photo by the author.

Green taro

GREEN TARO (***Colocasia esculenta***) - is usually a large plant growing to 42 inches tall. Performs equally well in full sun or shade. This plant is great for indoors and has "elephant ear" shaped leaves. It prefers 0 to 12 inches of water over it. Smaller taro plants can work well in tubs and kettles.

"Purple leaf taro"

"PURPLE LEAF TARO' (genus ***Colocasia***) - Imperial Taro and Black Princess Taro display purple and green colored leaves. These are large taro plants that perform equally well in full sun or shade and prefer 0 to 6 inches of water over. Some of these plants can grow about 42 inches tall.

Purple Leaf Taro, *Colocasia* **species. Photo by the author.**

FLOWERING MARGINALS

Red stemmed thalia

RED STEMMED THALIA (***Thalia geniculata*** forma ***ruminoides***) - This plant grows 5 feet tall with large, exotic, "banana-tree"-like leaves. The flowers are on spikes reaching heights of 8 to 10 feet. It prefers 0 to 6 inches of water over it and favors full sun or partial sun.

Water irises

WATER IRISES - These closely resemble the land iris varieties. Many water irises grow 15 to 18 inches tall (some reach 24 to 30 inches in height), favor full sun or partial sun, and prefer 0 to 6 inches of water over them. Blossoms can come in many colors including white, yellow, red, blue, and violet. There are many varieties of water irises available. Many of these water irises do very well in tubs and kettles.

Water canna

WATER CANNA - The water cannas strongly resemble the land canna varieties. Often, water canna flowers are vivid yellow, orange, and red accompanied by large, exotic, "banana-tree"-like leaves. Water cannas grow best in full sun with 0 to 6 inches of water over it.

Water hibiscus

WATER HIBISCUS (***Hibiscus coccinea***) - it is also known as "Lord Baltimore" hibiscus. This plant has huge 8 to 10 inch

Water Canna.

Red Stemmed Thalia, *Thalia geniculata* **forma** *ruminoides.* **Photo by the author at the Swift Family Garden Pools, Missouri Botanical Gardens.**

Left: Water Canna at the Missouri Botanical Gardens.

vivid red flowers and is a deciduous shrub that grows about 5 feet tall. It must be both water and winter protected. It comes from Australia.

Below left: Water Hibiscus, *Hibiscus coccinea*. Also called the Lord Baltimore Hibiscus. Photo by the author. Below right: Close up of the flowers of the Water Hibiscus, *Hibiscus coccinea*. Photo by the author

NATIONAL SUPPLIERS

Lilypons Water Gardens
P.O. Box 10
Buckeystown, MD 21717
1-800-999-5459 (Toll free orders)
1-800-999-LILY (Customer service)
Catalog-$5.00 (very colorful)
Hours of Operation:
9:30-5:30 all 7 days (March-October)
9:30-4:30 Mon-Sat (November-February)
Near Washington, DC
ALSO
Lilypons Water Gardens
P.O. Box 188
Brookshire, TX 77423
(Near Houston)

Slocum Water Gardens
1101 Cypress Gardens Blvd.
Winter Haven, FL 33884-1932
Catalog-$3.00 (very colorful)
1-941-293-7151
1-800-322-1896 (Fax orders)
(Near Orlando, FL)

Van Ness Water Gardens
2460 North Euclid Avenue
Upland, CA 91784
Catalog-$4.00 (very colorful)
1-909-982-2425
1-800-205-2425 (Order department)
Hours of Operation:
9:00-4:30 Tues.-Sat.
(Near Los Angeles)

Paradise Water Gardens
14 May Street
Whitman, MA 02382

Very colorful catalog
1-617-447-4711 and 1-617-447-8595
Near Brockton, MA)
AND
Stetson Aquatic Nursery
(Located near Paradise Water Gardens)

Perry's Water Gardens
191 Leatherman Gap Road
Franklin, NC 28734
1-704-524-3264
1-800-545-9723 (Order number)
Colorful catalog
Hours of Operation:
9:00-5:00 Mon.-Sat.
Display gardens open from May 20 through Labor Day

Scherer Water Gardens
104 Waterside Road
Northport, NY 11768
1-516-261-7432
Hours of Operationa:
8:00-6:00 Mon.-Sat.
9:00-4:00 Sunday
(Winter hours may vary)

The Water Works
111 East Fairmont Street
Coopersburg, PA 18036
1-610-282-4784
1-800-360-LILY (Order number)

Matterhorn Nursery, Inc.
227 Summit Park Road
Spring Valley, NY 10977
1-914-354-5986

The above information on the national water garden suppliers came from their own catalogs of 1998 and reflect the summer of 1997 prices. Hence, in succeeding years, some of the above information could change.

SUPPLIERS

When planning your water garden, be sure to contact at least several local suppliers and also national water garden suppliers to see what is available and at what prices. At the local level, suppliers include pet shops, aquarium stores, hardware stores, large discount stores, drug stores, agricultural supply stores, sand or gravel companies, equipment stores, local construction supply stores, and local nurseries. In many cases, the most reasonable prices of EPDM flexible liner are at the local roofing supply companies. If one needs help in excavating, one can check with local excavators, gravel companies, local nurseries, etc. At a local nursery, you can easily obtain useful information about starting water gardens. So, be sure to contact many suppliers before you start building your water garden. Also, be sure to contact the specialty national water garden suppliers as they often have very reasonable prices.

NATIONAL WATER GARDEN SUPPLIERS

National water garden suppliers are specialty suppliers of plants, supplies, and equipment for water gardens. In the past, my experience with specialty suppliers is that they are often overpriced. However, the national water garden suppliers are very competitive in most prices and should be considered as potential sources of supply. Their prices compare very favorably with local suppliers. In addition, some of these suppliers have toll free customer service numbers to ask advice. Their prices on water lilies, marginal plants, and other plants are very attractive. I'd recommend those starting in water gardening to order specific proven species of water lilies from these suppliers for the type of proposed pool and the climate of the area in which they live.

In addition, most of the following national water lily suppliers have outstanding display areas for their water lilies and other plants. If in their area, please feel free to stop and view their exotic plants. You may want to call first to see if their display gardens are viewable. The addresses, phone numbers, and in some cases the hours of operation of these national suppliers are given below.

COSTS

In my review of water lily literature, one of my biggest disappointments was the lack of information about the prices of water gardening supplies and equipment. Catalogues by the national water garden suppliers had this information available in many cases. Hence, at the back of certain chapters and at the end of this book are the prices I found for such items.

Remember that these prices reflect what I found in the summer of 1996 in Omaha, Nebraska. The supplied figures are for indications of possible costs. However, prices do vary for different sections of this country as well as the type of locality in which you live. It is the responsibility of the water gardener to find out what the actual costs would be regarding their pools. Also, as the years go by, I would expect the prices to go up. My figures again are in 1996 U.S. dollars.

In most cases, I have denoted the sourcing of my selected items with either an "L" or an "N." The "L" stands for a LOCAL source. The "N" stands for a NATIONAL water garden supplier source as per their catalogue.

TYPICAL PLANT COSTS

Type of plant

Horsetail	$7 - $9
Papyrus	$12 - $18
Dwarf Papyrus	$4 - $7.50
Common Cattail	$5.25 - $6
Purple Colored Taro (Leaf)	$10
Water Iris	$5 - $10
Water Canna	$10 - $13
Pickerel Weed (White Flower)	$3.50 - $5.25

WATER LILIES:

Hybrid Hardies	$18
Specific Hardy Species	$20 - $40
Specific Tropical Species	$21 - $40
Red Flare (a tropical)	$35 - $40
Helvola (a hardy)	$25 - $45
Fabiola (Pink Beauty) (a hardy)	$20 - $28
Colorata (a tropical)	$23 - $40
Dauben	$20 - $23

GENERAL COSTS

Small Backhoe (L)	$160-$200 per day
Excavation Labor (L)	$30 per man hour
Decorative Rock (Depends on color)(L)	10 to 22¢ per pound
Dirt (L)	$12 per cubic yard
Sand (L)	$16 per ton
Pea Gravel (L)	$37 per ton
EPDM Flexible Liner (45 mil) (L)	55¢-$1.38 per sq. ft.
(N)	74¢-99¢ per sq. ft.
PVC Flexible Liner (20 mil (L)	75¢ per sq. ft.
(N)	63¢-$1.05 per sq. ft.
PVC Flexible Liner (32 mil) (N)	81¢-85¢ per sq. ft.
Wooden Whiskey Half Barrel & Liner (L)	$50
Polyethylene Half Barrell (N)	$30-$33
Kettles (N)	$90-$135
Wheeled Storage Unit (45 Gallon) (L)	$30-$35
Aerating Pump (L) (N)	$45-$50
Chemicals to Fight Water Contaminants (N)	$8-$18
Feeder Goldfish (L)	20¢-25¢
Ramshorn Snails (for 6-9 snails) (N)	40¢-75¢
Ground Fault Circuit Interrupter (N)	$50-$70
De-icer with Guard (N)	$60
Pond Netting (N)	$10-$35
Pond Sweeps (N)	$27-$86
Water Removing Pumps (N)	$170-$200
Landscape Ties (L) 3" x3" x 8'	$5
	$2.72 (sale)
4" x4" x 12' Ties (L)	$13
24" x 18" Plastic Container (L)	$13.30-$15
14" x 12 1/4" Plastic Container (L)	$2
Rebar (Solid Metal Bar - 1/2" diam x 10') (L)	$2
Burlap (3'w x 48'1) (L) = $15	10.4¢ per sq. ft.
Fabric Mulch (in 6' wide rolls) (L)	15¢ per sq. ft.